Getting Out of the BOAT

ERIC CATRON

WESTBOW
PRESS®
A DIVISION OF THOMAS NELSON
& ZONDERVAN

WestBow Press books may be ordered through booksellers or by contacting:

WestBow Press
A Division of Thomas Nelson & Zondervan
1663 Liberty Drive
Bloomington, IN 47403
www.westbowpress.com
844-714-3454

ISBN: 978-1-6642-9699-2 (sc)
ISBN: 978-1-6642-9698-5 (e)

Print information available on the last page.

WestBow Press rev. date: 04/03/2023

CONTENTS

DEDICATION

I would like to first off, glorify God the Creator for applying His voice to this creation. If you know me, you would know I could hardly formulate a children's book let alone one of this nature.

My Wife Mandie, for the support, prayers, love and my two daughters DeziRae and Courtney who, well, just put up with me, I suppose, as teenagers.

My Pastor in crime and Brother in Christ Paul, you lift me up, frustrate me, laugh and cry with me and feel every ounce of my walk in the valley's. We will be celebrating soon on the mountain top, my friend. (Picture edition coming.) Pastor Brad for being my prayer warrior through all the battles. Thank you.

My Church family, you provide support and encouragement in tough times and you are always on your knees praying for my recovery and my ministry.

My editor, Tammy, whom I have laughed with
over the years, cried with and here recently opt
to wring her neck for her overzealous editing
abilities. Other,, THAN,, that,, who knows.
;-) You are a blessing in so many ways.

My community, the church extends far beyond
those four walls, you continually reach out to
support my efforts and pray for my needs.

My Mother and Sister who got excited every time
I sent them a new revision to preview. Along
with your support during my health ordeals
and constant prayers, I am forever grateful.

All my family and friends for being there, physically,
emotionally and in whatever capacity I may require.
You're a solid foundation that was built upon a rock!

I certainly cannot forget my Oncology and
Cardiac teams and hospital staff who have
afforded me life with their Christ-like touch.

God bless you all.

FOREWORD

When Eric told me in March of this year (2019) that he was writing a book and –more importantly- intended to have it completed in a month, I did not believe him. Sincerely, I thought he was the king of wishful thinking.

You see, I have authored a few books in my time (all fiction, none as involved as this), and I am acutely aware of how long it takes to write a book. This is not an endeavor that takes weeks, or even months; sometimes it takes years.

I remember I nodded and smiled and said something along the lines of, "That's fantastic! I'm excited to read it!" Because, you see, I am a supportive friend, and Eric has supported me through some very difficult times as well.

And Eric was fighting cancer.

And Eric had just survived a heart attack.

And, to be honest, Eric was not looking well.

He was pale, tired looking; worn you might say. His voice was weak, but his spirit- that was as strong as I have ever seen it.

Somehow, in the midst of our conversation, Eric had recruited me to edit this piece of literature. Of course, I agreed. Again, Eric is my friend and there was nothing he could have asked me at that point that I wouldn't have at least considered attempting.

So Eric sent me the first few chapters- by few I mean seven- SEVEN chapters he had already written; following a heart attack; while fighting cancer.

I read the first few chapters, skimmed actually, if I were to be honest; I really wasn't expecting big things- sorry Eric. Then somewhere around the third chapter I found myself being sucked in. This was unusual, because I generally don't read a lot of non-fiction. I don't do self-help books, inspiration books, life-altering sagas; I do murder mysteries. Side note- this was a subject that came up when Eric and I talked about my editing- I remember telling him, "Hey, I'm a fiction reader and writer- I don't do self-help and I'm not a minister, priest, preacher, etc. Are you SURE you want *me* to edit this?" But Eric was confident and his confidence made me confident.

I stopped skimming and went back and started *reading*- an important distinction- and quickly realized this was gold. For someone who- and I quote, "…is not a grammatically correct writer and I'm supper happy you see through that…" and is a "…meanderererer…" Eric had begun writing something incredible. Something that I daresay speaks to the general population, not just those entering the ministry in an official type capacity, but those who minister in any manner. Further, it is a compelling read.

Eric sent me the first chapters of his book March 23, 2019, and while I began editing those, he continued working, oftentimes writing while he was at chemo. There were times he really cranked things out and I could NOT keep up with him- particularly when his steroids were upped. There were times his neuropathy posed an additional challenge because his fingers would freeze on the keyboard sticking down a key, resulting in a number of spaces, multiple same letters, or periods……. and I would have to catch those and fix them.

Sometimes the order of his thoughts would come in a jumble and it was extra difficult for me to make sense of what he meant and try to place it in correct order. He had SO many thoughts and they were flying at him more quickly than his hindered fingers could type.

Eric and I communicated multiple times daily over the last week of March and all through April, and we became quite the team. Whenever I doubted myself, Eric was there to bolster me- ME. His health was consistently on shaky ground, but he was more concerned with how I was doing and making sure I knew he trusted me implicitly in regards to editing this book. One day (when I was desperately trying to keep up with his rapid progress), he texted me saying: "Please feel free to revise as your (yes I know- he said your) able I trust you and know God will move just as well through you too." That message became far more important than he ever realized it would.

Eric was right; he finished his book in a month. And I sincerely believe with every part of my existence that God breathed it through him. Eric's part was done and he passed away April 29, 2019. I do not know how many more things Eric completed and was supposed to complete before his passing, so I cannot speak to those, but this one thing I was a part of, and I believe this was something he was supposed to do. With God, all things are possible.

His passing made it incredibly difficult for me to continue editing. Without his input, his clarifications, I struggled to get in touch with his writing again. Then one day I was reviewing our many text conversations and I came across his message- God will move just as well through you too. I began praying on it, spilling out all of my concerns, my self-doubt, and my feelings of letting everyone- primarily his family- down. I asked God for guidance and Eric for help. I needed to hear his voice again. And then one day I did. As I told his wife, Eric's voice came back (and he didn't shut up) and suddenly we were a team again. After weeks of forcing myself to try and edit but really just spinning my wheels, in less than a week I had completed the final editing and it felt right for the first time. Thank you Eric!

The last thing I want to mention, is that you may notice in the beginning of the book- the part that is primarily focused on Eric's testimony, the telling is somewhat rough, does have some grammatical errors (much like his messages I have shared above), but I have deliberately left them that way, because I feel the resonance of Eric's voice through the wording, and I feel the reader will also hear that voice. It also creates a nice understanding of who Eric was as a person. When he is telling his own testimony- his personal story- it's a bit choppy- partly because I had to draw SO much of that out of him, because Eric, by nature, didn't really talk a lot about himself, he talked about you and your needs. Eric was wonderful in his role as a supporter, a teacher, and a guidance counselor- and this will instantly be noticeable once you reach the middle of this book and Eric steps into his comfy Pastoral shoes.

I will forever be changed by this experience, this book has lit a fire within me that, combined with other experiences I have had this year, has altered a lot about me, about how I think and who I am, and possibly my direction in life- God will let me know I am sure. And I will forever be grateful for the friendship and support Eric extended to me; may you rest in peace my friend, I love you.

God bless you all. Tammy Ingham

INTRODUCTION

Have you ever wondered how people knew they were called into ministry? Matthew 28:19-20 New King James Version (NKJV) "Go therefore and make disciples of all the nations, baptizing them in the name of the Father and of the Son and of the Holy Spirit, teaching them to observe all things that I have commanded you; and lo, I am with you always, even to the end of the age." That may seem strange for someone that has never been introduced to ministry work and may leave a lot of questions unanswered.

I remember when I entered the ministry several years ago it was an exciting and scary time. I did not know what to expect, who to turn to, or even how to go about the process. All I felt was a tug to do it. A tug can be confusing if you have never felt an emotional tug on your spirit before. It's like an intuition or a strong urge, and whether you're supposed to act upon it may depend on how strong the urge is felt. Throughout this book I will make every effort to share the variety of thoughts, feelings and responses I have experienced and, to the best that I am able, attempt to describe what led up to what I believe created that tug within me to enter ministry. In ministry often we refer to this experience as a testimony, transformation, or getting saved (accepting the Lord as your Savior, or becoming born again, in my case). There is a growth process that takes place when one is "saved". My belief is that once you become saved, you are in ministry; otherwise a complete transformation may not have blossomed yet.

Before I felt the calling to enter ministry, I was very much of the world as many are, thinking in my terms, not God pleasing terms. What's more interesting, I had very little knowledge of who God was and what He had in store for me. I was raised around a few people that went to church, but that was all it was, people that went to church. I saw church clergy dressed in gowns, blessing things and making offerings. I had others telling me when to sit, stand, and kneel in order to fulfill some sort of spiritual obligation I didn't understand but assumed was taking place. When services dismissed, the crowd would make their way to the local restaurants and establishments, and behave no differently than when they first attended the meeting that morning. There would be discord at the tables- loud, shouting arguments- and patrons demanding unreasonable things from their wait staff. These observations would make me want to spit in their cheeseburgers if I had been the one serving them. (I know, yuck!)

If church wasn't going to help someone be a better person, then why get up so early and go, I thought. Better to sleep in, watch cartoons, eat donuts and drink chocolate milk, right? (Anybody remember Moose and Squirrel or the Mystery Machine? Remember, I was young then, I've since had to give that up. I only watch cartoons now- no chocolate milk- lactose intolerant!)

Religion was quite the turn off, pointless (except for the Pope's hat), and a waste of time. After all, wasn't church supposed to be where lives got changed? I picked up on that even at a very early pre-teen age. Can you imagine what my early adult years would assimilate? I had no desire to be a part of the church or what it stood for. Much better things lay in wait for me to do on any precious given Sunday.

Let's look at how it all began to change. Please understand, it doesn't happen the same way for everyone, but as I mentioned earlier, what you will find here is a mix of questions, concerns and thoughts that formulated during my personal journey into serving the Lord. Perhaps some affirmation for what you could be experiencing too. Before proceeding, let me also highlight that my transformation was not an all-out, "God completely transformed my life in one single glimmering moment!" My transformation comes in the form of several portions of testimony spread out over the course of a few events and a timeframe spanning a couple of years. As mentioned also, I knew God, I knew who He was, but my relationship was not what today I would call being a "Christian" or being "saved." So keep that in mind as we learn, explore my heart and grow together.

My prayer is that you find value in this reference to validate what you are feeling and allow God to move you where those feelings take you. Let's venture on and have some fun.

MY STORY

EVERYBODY HAS ONE, A STORY THAT MAKES YOU WHO YOU ARE. LAST chapter we called this a testimony. So why is your story important to consider when that spiritual tug is felt on your spirit? For me, it was a discovery process of who I was and who I wanted to be after a course of events took place that altered my life.

The first 30 plus years of my life were what I would call secular years, years in which very little I did or worked for was pleasing to God, but was very rewarding to me. Let's call it an "I" problem and as I saw it, it harmed no one. I was successful in my career endeavors, I made great money and had lots of friends who encouraged my habits-spiraling habits, that is. It would be several more years before I would understand that and the impact that it would have on my life.

Born and raised in middle class suburban America with all the American traditions to boot, life seemed great. Military years brought even more validation to my ever-expanding ego, along with a few extra unwanted claims such as drinking, irresponsible financial management and an overall reckless attitude towards the lives and well-being of others or me.

Moving to the Midwest seemed to discourage some of those irresponsible worldly behaviors, but they continued to linger in my mind and always seemed to stir in the background of who I was at the core and where my life had been wasted. Three marriages later life seemed to begin to have meaning and more valuable purpose. Children tend to do that to you, I suppose.

My lifelong passion and career in the automotive business, which had proved well for me financially, seemed to be coming, by choice, to an end as I began exploring options in a less physically demanding environment. Fields that really touched my heart became a bigger focus. I wasn't getting any younger and it was, after all, a physically demanding job standing on concrete and lifting, pulling and prying automotive parts around a vehicle all day. While I enjoyed the challenge of fixing vehicles with all the modern technology being thrown into them, something inside of me was saying it was time for a change.

I always had an interest in cyber-crimes investigation, especially in the field of missing and exploited children. At that time, the internet underworld really seemed to be coming alive with predators and crimes against innocent children. The world was just starting to realize how much of a threat internet safety was regarding the welfare of children and the unsuspecting. With all these predators popping up all over the place I became almost instantly driven to pursue this new passion.

Adult continuing education, a.k.a. college, seemed inevitable and while hitting the books seemed like a big hurdle to tackle at this stage in my life, I had a burning desire to get involved with cyber-crimes investigation work and that is exactly what I was going to do. Two years into a Bachelor's in Criminal Justice, and thousands of dollars in student loan debt, something happened (besides the debt collection calls), and it wasn't good. It was close, it was personal, and it hurt.

My father's health was in jeopardy.

My father, who lived on the East coast, had been ill and was in urgent need of medical intervention. I hurried home to be by his side as he underwent operation after operation in an effort to treat a bad case of pancreatitis. It was during that time that the tug I mentioned earlier in this book began to materialize through an interesting set of events that took place.

One afternoon while I was down in the hospital gift shop I ran across a book called, "90 *Minutes in Heaven,*" by Pastor Don Piper. For some reason, unknown to me at the time, I took an immediate interest in it. A little insight into the book: a pastor, Don Piper, was involved in a serious head on car crash that took his life. He spent some time in Heaven and was able to come back in an almost impossible set of circumstances. The rest tells the story behind his heavenly experiences and recovery. A nearly impossible situation to survive turned into a blessing to so many able to experience his testimony.

I purchased the book and took it upstairs to begin the long arduous process of reading. (Yes, that was my take on the task at the time.) To my surprise, I finished it within three days and something had begun to grow inside of me, a question, an itch to know more, to dig deeper.

Thankfully, my father's health seemed to take a turn for the better and I felt comfortable returning home to my soon-to-be-wife and kids. A week later I received a call in the middle of the night. My father had passed away. It was a blow too hard to bear. I headed back to the East coast once more, this time nursing the deep hurt I was experiencing at the loss of my father, but also with very different feelings about God and why this had happened at such a young age to my father and his family. I had lots of questions.

The passing of my father had a tremendous impact on me. We were do-it-yourself buddies, bouncing around home-improvement ideas, yard projects and crafts as well; we loved to work with our hands, though the physical distance between us had put some guilt and strain on that relationship. I assume 600 miles can have that type of impact on a relationship sometimes.

Then something new to me began to occur... I bought my first adult Bible and began to read it. Within days of that wrapper coming off I found myself writing my father's eulogy in an effort to not only make sense of what had happened, but to also, in some way, honor his life and search for an ounce of peace in my own.

The eulogy was cried over by many in attendance that cold winter day, but oddly a sense of awe and wonder came over me. Let's call this a presence of peacefulness that I would later put words to, but at the time (still a bit angry with God) I had no words for. Sure, I was sad that I had suddenly lost my father in this tragic way, but I had something guarding me against the spiraling effect a traumatic event such as this can have on a person.

Time went by, but not much, and next on the list of events about to impact my life was my wedding.

Only thirty days from laying my father to rest, I would be marrying my third and final wife, a true blessing and certainly a part of my testimony worth mentioning. My father was not going to be there. We would do everything possible to honor his spiritual presence with us that special day, but I wouldn't hear him utter the words, "I am proud of you son, for who you have become," though I knew he was. I suppose it's one of those things when you lay your head on the pillow at night and ask questions and seek answers from an unfamiliar entity or god that you are just skimming the surface of getting to know and you're not too sure of.

As we all know, life goes on, as did my wedding, and I was more blessed then I could ever have imagined. My life, work and family were taking on a new and much more dynamic part of my world. Life was getting better. It was good and yet that tug was still there maturing, waiting to come alive even more inside of me. Did I put those feelings aside or was God still preparing me at this point? By the end of this book I think you will strategically find the answer within yourself.

Here is where it gets crazy (we will eventually begin to call these God moments). Still working through my schooling in Criminal Justice, I landed a fun job as a loss prevention detective for a local retail chain. Due to some unfortunate, yet timely (God thing) circumstances, I was managing the department in less than three months and having a blast playing mall cop. I had an amazing team of detectives that I bonded with and they held a special place in my heart. (Two of them were even a couple of them "CHRISTIANS".) Outside of their beautiful personalities, it was never pushed to make me feel uncomfortable. (Thanks Jen and Billy, forever in your debt for what was about to transpire.)

I was coaching my youth soccer team one warm summer evening when my cell phone kept ringing. Being the devoted coach, I kept silencing it in fairness to my team responsibilities. It was relentless, so I finally gave in and picked up. The voice on the other end was my beautiful sister in Christ, Jen. She was contacting me to tell me she had arranged a very special weekend that would change my life forever and I had to go home to get ready. (If you know Jen, you know that you can't say no and live.) I had less than thirty minutes to arrive at this "mystery event" that was supposed to "transform my life" and I had already attempted every excuse to get myself out of it, to no avail. I explained I had to work the rest of the week. Covered already, boss. We have a game this weekend, I reasoned. Assistant coach has already got it covered. I tried saying there was no way my wife would let me go away for whole weekend while she was stuck at home with the kids. It's all good, boss. Defeated! That's where I was. So, with my head hung low, I went and experienced, to my astonishment, God, first hand.

Now it's hard to put into words exactly what happened that weekend I met God, or drew closer to God, but here is my attempt. The weekend, call it a retreat, was organized by individuals that had at one time all gone through the same process that was going to occur for us newcomers. There was a group of attendees like myself that either knew God and were not saved, or were as far from God as they could get and desperately needed something more in their lives. Their "sponsors," such as my Jen and Billy, were able to arrange to make this retreat happen for them, just as my sponsors had made it happen for me. The group of men organized talks (testimonies style), encouragement, and listening to our problems in an intervention style of drawing meaning and purpose out of God in our lives. Quiet reflection time, fellowship and much, much more I am not even supposed to mention as to not spoil it for others. So, I won't. Just mind you, it was amazing. The last activity after a very emotionally draining weekend was to make a decision that would change our lives forever. On the last evening at the retreat I experienced that tug, and it was undeniably felt, and it shook me to the core and beyond. I gave over my life to Christ, "got saved," "was born again," "became a child of God." However, you want to spin the term, I was on fire with the desire to know Him much more than ever before.

Now you have to remember what I had just experienced for the last 72 hours non-stop and when I returned home that Sunday I found the world hadn't changed by Monday morning. Reality still existed; the world is often a brutal, harsh environment. My new reality was the need for others to experience what I had experienced. I wanted others to undergo the same transformation of the heart that I had, to no longer experience the reality of the world without being equipped to maneuver within it. And there lies the basis for my move towards ministry. A heart transplant of my own occurred, then a deep desire to transform others. A few other things transpired completing the cycle, but I opted to save those for another section.

GOD'S TIMING

I F YOU'RE LIKE ME, THE WORD OF GOD WASN'T A BEST SELLER THAT WAS sitting on your book shelf. I, on the other hand, was collecting Cyber Crime documents and books, attending seminars on interviewing and investigation techniques and courts and law procedures.

I was sitting at work one day, an environment which included a couple dozen nine inch black and white monitors, a few large screens, and a couple control joysticks to move the cameras around. An 'apprehension' began, involving a younger individual who appeared to have some serious problems. So, my team and I set out to do what we did best, "Stop, thief, stop!" All too often, getting the adolescent back to the office was an interesting venture. Fear and emotion were usually at the forefront of every thought and action they made. Typically, unless they were regulars, their response prompted a fight or flight mentality. Perhaps some of the fear came from not knowing what was going to happen to them. This particular encounter seemed to be noticeably intensified for some reason.

On the way back to the detention room a very long and intense conversation began, one full of tears and apologies. The more questions I asked, the more I saw something broken inside of him, something desperate to get out. Out it got. Everything that was wrong in his world came bubbling to a head and I did something I had never done before. I sat quietly and listened while it all happened.

When his face finally reappeared from the shelter of his arms folded on my desk, in lieu of the typical, "Please don't call my parents, they'll kill me," conversation, a real conversation began. The more we interacted, the more I observed something in him that gave me pause. Something that made me ask, "Have you experienced something that made you become more emotional than normal? Know this, it isn't a bad thing, you just remind me a lot of myself."

His reply overwhelmed me with an authoritative, "Yes! And then something bad happened to me that I didn't understand."

I became exceedingly curious. Had he met Jesus, like I had? (At the time, everything to me seemed to revolve around Jesus, so Jesus popped up in every thought I had and to this day it quite often still does. Well, most every thought.) My assumption at this point was that he was under attack, and I didn't understand why. Just as I had observed the Monday after my Jesus intervention, nothing had seemed pleasing, as if the world was attacking somehow. That weekend experience, "The Jesus encounter," had been all about love, then I had stepped back into a world that wasn't, its reality was harsh, cold, even cruel. Do I dare step as far out as evil? I do. When you experience genuine love from God it tends to feel that way. The love still exists, but now seems infiltrated by so many other things. If you could imagine spending a month at the "Happiest place on earth," (otherwise known as Disney World), then suddenly return to the daily grind of life, you would feel a bit disappointed and defeated, maybe even attacked. In ministry, we call those mountain top experiences and valleys. I am certain you can discern the difference. So, I was still wondering, was this kid being attacked in the same way I had felt the Monday after my mountain top experience?

Then Jesus was led up by the Spirit into the
wilderness to be tempted by the devil. (Matt 4:1)

I haven't unpacked a lot of scripture in this book yet because, if you're like me, scripture can be intimidating at first. So, our approach with scripture will be progressing throughout the book to help ease the transition. After all, this book is about entering the ministry, not simply falling on your face in agony. So let's take a brief moment and look at the above scripture to see what was going on in Jesus's world at the time.

Jesus, the God of the world, the Son of mankind, was tempted. There you have it! Why you ask? He was a threat; a threat to everything Satan was trying to accomplish. Satan knew that Jesus was the answer to the world's problems, and he was bound and determined to not let that happen. So just before the scripture tells us that Jesus's ministry began, He was tempted. More on that later.

Since this kid had been introduced to God, it began to dawn on me that it could possibly be a similar situation to that which Jesus had experienced and Satan's army had begun to take every effort to prevent the kid from following God closer.

Don't tell anyone, but I ended up letting that boy go home as if nothing had ever happened. Usually I can see through their feeble attempts at lying their way out of an arrest, but this one felt different inside of me and well, it was just a pair of earrings.

That tug...yeah, I felt it, and God had prepared my heart to the point where I wanted more and more of those encounters and was even trying to turn normal encounters into mighty spiritual encounters. Often with ill-mannered responses, but I didn't care. I became hungry to do this and to seek out opportunities. God's timing was beginning, and it wasn't because an angel came down upon a boulder, lit a bush on fire and told me to lead the people. He just allowed me to taste the need that was around me and I was open to it. Do you think prior to that weekend experience I had meeting up with God and giving my life to Him that this would have been possible? I don't believe so. It was a desire to be and act more like Jesus that prompted these new feelings I was experiencing inside of me. This craving was far beyond the tug and difficult at this point to explain. So, we will sit on that feeling for now.

I don't recall the exact date things began to make the significant shift from criminal justice to ministry. God just said to me, "Take a

Bible class." It was literally one phone call to my current college to cancel classes and then to another to a different college to reregister. After all, I had no formal ministry training or education. God was about to put all that into my lap. Since I still had a family to feed and bills to pay, I needed to figure out how this was going to work. There is that 'I' problem I referred to earlier. The 'I' problem is the fact that *I* am still trying to be in control of what happens, instead of the Lord. Well, He did it anyway. I still took the credit, but the Lord would soon open a door to Hospice ministry (helping those who are terminally ill find quality and meaning of life). It was a chaplain job that didn't seem like a big deal, but those types of jobs don't just fall out of the sky like manna from the heavens, and the position it placed me in was God's timing, I would later learn.

There I was, immersed in a new world with a lot of opportunity to do good for people and the Lord. God's timing. There was no searching; God just aligned it all to fall into place because it was not something I was able to do. Who in their right mind would let someone with very little working chaplaincy experience just come in and start ministering to families in need in a Hospice setting?

If I were to rewind just a little bit, I had started attending a church that only believed in sharing what the word of God said. The minister of that Church had retired from the very position I would soon be taking over. Again, God's timing. Perhaps, if you haven't gotten the hint yet, allow God to move you where He wants you. He will, since you are His child. He won't let you sit idle while the enemy stirs all around us.

If you think God is trying to do just that and you are still not sure, then there is a good possibility that you are still trying to be at the helm and be in control of what happens. Be vulnerable and open to what God is trying to do. He may tell you through one of those little whispers in your ear to go sit at a fast food establishment and buy someone's lunch. He may have you volunteer a few hours at a food pantry. Your ministry may be doing something in homeless shelters. He is waiting to whisper to you, "This is what I want you to do, to prepare yourself to serve me better."

God's timing is not our own, but it is perfect timing.

In the beginning God created the heavens
and the earth. (Genesis 1, NKJV)

Thus, the heavens and the earth, and all the host
of them, were finished. And on the seventh day
God ended His work which He had done, and
He rested on the seventh day from all His work
which He had done. (Genesis 2:1-2, NKJV)

These passages show God in His six days of timing aligned everything for life to exist perfectly designed. His word proceeds to tell us that on that seventh day he rested. He did not mention retiring, or falling into a two or three-thousand year sleep while man came along to keep that perfect creation going. He rested and most certainly got back to work, continuing with His creation. A little off course here, but think about it, if this is true, as new scientific findings continue to reveal unexplored galaxies and solar systems that exist, if God had a need for us to know about what He was working on now, He would have told us. God may have just said, "Hey, I'll be back on Monday to continue working on this creation thing, just wanted to take a break for a day and rest up because those platypuses were difficult to keep in line when I made them." Okay, that paragraph was free.

My point is God is continually working, attentive to all of His Creations. And His timing, His perfect design for which we have all been created, and His perfect plan for our lives, exists. Our part is where we decide to listen and allow it to happen for us. You have a perfect plan waiting for you to discover. One final piece of evidence of this to share:

"Before I formed you in the womb I knew you;
Before you were born I sanctified you;
I ordained you a prophet to the
nations." Jeremiah 1:5 (NKJV)

Don't worry if that wording sounds odd or unfamiliar. It simply means you're His child and His deepest desire is to use you.

3

THE GOSPEL

P ERHAPS NOTHING I WRITE IN THIS BOOK IS MORE IMPORTANT THAN THIS section. When I say important, I mean not only for the purpose of this book, but for the purpose of life. The Gospel, or "Good news," is the heartbeat of our existence. Eternity will happen regardless, the only saving factor is location, location, location. It's a lot like real estate that way. Whether or not you have confirmed the Gospel message in your heart, will determine where that location ends up being. There is a rather humorous saying, "Sanctified or chicken fried." Well, I suppose that depends on which end of the spectrum you're looking at.

Now please take note that I did not elaborate on the process of confirming the Gospel message in our hearts. My purpose in writing this book is not to bring doctrinal disputes and denominational barriers to the forefront. If you are at a place in your life where you are uncertain of your salvation, perhaps you are not hearing from the Creator in the first place. There is still a chance your God is speaking to you, but I urge you at this place in your life to be absolutely certain He is. It is not a message you want to accept lightly. It is important to grasp this no matter how excited you are at the possibilities of doing something you feel passionate about. Take this into consideration first, please.

"And another sign appeared in heaven: behold, a great, fiery red dragon having seven heads and ten horns, and seven diadems on his heads. His tail drew a third of the stars of heaven and threw them to the earth. And the dragon stood before the woman who was ready to give birth, to devour her Child as soon as it was born." Revelation 12:3-4 NKJV

I have injected this scripture to help show the power the enemy (Satan) has over an individual. It isn't hard for us as humans to simply lean back and imagine what heaven is like, after all, there are a plethora of books, documents, and even living testimony of people that have died and entertained a place in heaven for a period- and Hell also. If you're curious do a web-search of the topic. If what we envision heaven to be like does it any justice, just imagine the power of influence a single angel must have had to have been able to deceive a third of God's angels to leave the perfection of heaven?

As a working Pastor I have been increasingly cognizant of the power that surrounds me in the spiritual realm. As a new believer the attacks can wage a higher impact from the spiritual realm. We are not talking about Ghost Busters type stuff; we are talking about Good versus Evil, God versus Satan. I have access to a host of tools in my arsenal. No tool is more powerful than God's word itself. The power to heal, to move mountains, to calm storms and more, all originating from our call on faith in God being the God He is: all loving, all powerful and with all ability.

"Grace and peace be multiplied to you in the knowledge of God and of Jesus our Lord, as His divine power has given to us all things that pertain to life and godliness, through the knowledge of Him who called us by glory and virtue, by which have been given to us exceedingly great and precious promises, that through these you may be partakers of the divine nature, having escaped the corruption that is in the world through lust." II Peter 1:2-4 NKJV

The passage from II Peter 1 says that we are partakers of the divine nature. The power of the divine is available to us. Did you read that? The power that began the process of creation is at our disposal. So, what is the divine? That gets interpreted as the highest of powers, the creator of the universe, the one capable of all things to exist and to happen. The divine is God, himself, Jesus and the Holy Spirit of God. Never discredit the power that exists there and that which also has been afforded upon His children, you and I.

What does all this mean? It means that if we don't equip ourselves with all the powers available to us, we can easily fall victim to the threats that surround us, threats such as deception, corruption, confusion, anger, frustration. By Spiritual definition we could say a threat is anything that removes our thoughts or sights from Jesus. The more threat we are to Satan and his plan, the more we are susceptible. That both scares me and motivates me to no end, and you will find out why in the following chapter.

The next reason I propose the Gospel as an important aspect of our journey is because without knowing who Jesus the Christ is, how can we draw close to Him and have any level of intimacy? Jesus is His name, Christ is His title. Just as there is an anti-Christ (Satan), we are blessed to be secured by a Christ who loves us and died for us.

Knowing Christ is important. For example, if we don't know our spouse, how can we possibly know what bothers them or makes them happy? I certainly would not want to be in a relationship with a stranger. Intimacy connects people together. Intimacy unites people's souls for a common purpose. If Jesus was speaking to you, would you still have the Sunday night football game on or would you turn it off to ensure He has your full undivided attention and everything He said was understood?

Jesus says to follow Him, what does that even look like? Are you willing to follow somebody that you have no idea what is involved in the process? Getting to know the Gospel means getting to know how Jesus lived, breathed and loved everything God created. It becomes learning how to forgive far beyond what seems imaginable in our world, but is required of us. The Gospel means loving your enemies while they persecute you, being selfless in all that you set out to do. The Gospel means so much more than this introduction to ministry book has afforded time for. (Maybe the next movement of God in my life could be to document something that could contain that material.) But for now, The Gospel: live it, breath it, know it, and Him, and forever follow it. If this book were to stop right here, you would have enough information to be successful not only in ministry, but in life as well. But wait, there's more, but you gotta act now! We won't double your order, but we sure can bless you with God's graces upon you.

4

DISCERNMENT

O KAY, SO WE MOVED ON TO WORDS AND DEFINITIONS FOR A MOMENT. Discernment: it's just a bigger word to mean understand, or the ability to understand well in a spiritual sense of guidance. In other words, are you truly hearing the voice of God? Are you able to interpret God's intentions with a situation you have been placed in, or a conversation taking place between you and someone else? Are you being deceived by something yet still more powerful than you can take on?

God will never speak against His truth documented in His love story to us (The Bible). Therefore, it is extremely important to get an early start on knowing Him through his written word. After the Babylonian Exile (6th century BCE) and especially from the 3rd century BCE, Judaism became a more universal religion versus a localized one and God's origin name, Elohim, became more of a sovereignty of Israel over all other gods. (Big word break- sovereignty: power or complete authority over.) God's name was so spiritual, so holy, that the prophets and people of the time would not even speak His name, in order to preserve its sacred value, or they would use acceptable replacements such as YHWH. For the purpose of this material, YHWH becomes a fragmented piece of the origin word, Yahweh, a Hebrew word for God. Again, the material intended for this book does not allocate room for such a lengthy topic in and of itself. You will, however, notice throughout this book and others, that the word god, if capitalized, refers to the God of the Bible and that any lower-case reference god speaks merely of a god of some nature, not recognized as the origin Creator.

It is also important to understand that all scripture is God breathed and infallible (by definition mistake free), which comes to humanity without error or fault of any kind. It is a trustworthy and true document that, although we may disagree with a piece of content, we cannot call God a liar for revealing it to us. It is His word. There is a process our historical scribes took to painstakingly reproduce and preserve the accuracy and holiness of each documented page, long before PDF scanners and Word documents came to life. It was a process of precise duplication whereby during the verification process of a page if select positions of words (geographically centered words for example) did not align precisely with the original document it would be scrapped and started all over. This was a sometimes painstaking and lengthy process consuming months of time for one single page or recording of multiple copies. This only reveals the importance and reverence of the scriptures to the early scribes of this time. (So, you best be believing it's the real McCoy.)

Why is all this important? Again, you will be dealing with eternity. If you're a realtor you certainly wouldn't want to buy an ocean front retirement home that doesn't exist where advertised, but instead lies at the bottom of the ocean, would you? Not too appealing. You want that undeniable piece of eternity that guarantees you and your family in the heavens with the Creator. A view from the heavens: such a majestic and powerful image to take in. This only comes from knowing God, knowing His purpose for you, and not being deceived by the enemy's rendition.

I did mention to you that Satan is an Angel still, just a fallen one. Satan spent time in God's presence and knows a good portion of what God has revealed to us through scripture. And because of this, the great deceiver (Satan) is now able to twist words that God claims infallible just as He did in the garden planting doubt into God's desires for His children (read the fall of man in Genesis). My point with all this talk about Satan is if we are not equipped to discern the truth, to separate lies from the Word of God, then we are helpless prey in the hands of

Satan. Satan will deploy tactics onto us that look like they come from God Himself, but in fact are merely designed to snatch people into the darkness of Satan's territory. We must get to know Him and His word. Discernment is as important at the beginning while seeking out ministry as it is walking someone into the arms of Christ for the very first time. Placing heavy emphasis on the fact that the only way to know is to know Him and His truth.

While it is important to know all of God's written revelations through scripture, most Pastors (including myself) will tell you start with knowing Jesus in the New Testament first, and then dig in to the history of the Old Testament. You will quickly read that:

"Jesus said to him, "I am the way, the truth,
and the life. No one comes to the Father
except through Me." JOHN 14:6 NKJV

If you have been a slow reader all your life, and you start with the Old Testament, six months to a year may have gone by before you get to this vital piece of information found in the New Testament. This scripture reveals to us an important step into heaven through Jesus, the Christ of New Testament. Knowing the truth is important, but knowing the late breaking and newly released news is more important. Once you see God's character revealed to you through His son Jesus Christ, you will find you will be able to see God revealed through the Old Testament lens a whole lot easier and it will all come together. The Bible is the ultimate love story for His children and an instruction manual for life. The Bible says we will not know when Jesus returns for His children, although it's important to share the Gospel now, versus in six months to a year of getting through the Old Testament. It could make a big difference in some soul's ultimate location sooner than we would like.

This book will never make any effort to lessen the value of one particular piece of scripture, but in the face of an eternal clock, we must understand the value of the truth that shall set mankind free as quickly as possible so we can begin to share the Good News (Gospel) with the lost. Knowing the Gospel first allows you to do just that, share Jesus.

Discernment allows the spirit of God to reveal truth to you when we may not always know the answers. Discernment allows us to bind the mouth of the enemy from speaking through or to us when we instead know what God's character would have said. Remember, with discernment, God's love will always be revealed, not any form of deceptiveness or modified versions of it.

If you are still unfamiliar with how to discern God's love, turn to some resources. Today not only do we have the ability to read the Bible in many translated forms producing various reading styles but same end results, but we also have access to word studies of the Bible through faithful Bible scholars, secular institutions, online library resources and a host of internet provided resources. Take the time to do a long (but worth the effort) word study on the topic of love in the Bible, God's love, or others such as forgiveness, redemption, sanctification. It will get your mind discerning in the right direction. John 3:16-17 should be "industry standard," in other words, it should be the first verse that comes into consideration. Author's opinion injected, but I don't stand alone on this.

"For God so loved the world that He gave His only begotten Son, that whoever believes in Him should not perish but have everlasting life. For God did not send His Son into the world to condemn the world, but that the world through Him might be saved." John 3:16-17

Please do not let anyone remove John 3:17 from this memory life verse. John 3:17 reveals that God is of love, never desiring to harm anyone through this process of salvation. He is not a judge coming to wave a crooked finger, but a pair of arms coming to wrap around a hurting and lost soul. That is discerning the difference between a loving God and a God Satan will claim seeking out those to "send" to hell for eternity.

Ministry is not science, but you will find most decisions a minister will make are based on a Father's love. Discipline, affection and hard times are all part of God's love, but never meant to be traveled alone. The church is there to always edify fellow believers in Christ Jesus. Another fun word- edify or edification: to lift up, support, encourage. (We all need this by the way.)

5

MY FINAL LEAP

THIS, PERHAPS, WILL BECOME MY FAVORITE AND MOST EMOTIONAL chapter of this blessing consumers may call "Just another Christian book."

For me, what you are about to experience will hopefully motivate you to cry, laugh and move closer to God than ever. I believe people are placed in environments not necessarily as reward or punishments, but placed there to ultimately glorify God through their actions.

"And we know that all things work together for good to those who love God, to those who are the called according to His purpose" Romans 8:28 NJKV

Concerning this thing I pleaded with the Lord three times that it might depart from me. And He said to me, "My grace is sufficient for you, for My strength is made perfect in weakness." Therefore, most gladly I will rather boast in my infirmities, that the power of Christ may rest upon me. Therefore, I take pleasure in infirmities, in reproaches, in needs, in persecutions, in distresses, for Christ's sake. For when I am weak, then I am strong. 2 Corinthians 12:8-10 NKJV

Now there are numerous verses I could share to reveal what God has done with me as of lately. A pivotal piece of my journey began at the end of September of 2017. I, along with a few minister friends had been attending a minister gathering with the sole purpose of the group just to edify (lift each other up and care for each other as the Bible asks of us). We often call them spiritual retreats. Regardless, it was once again as in the past a beautiful Lord anointed weekend spent with good friends from around the world, not just the United States. A group of dynamic and humble men loving every moment they get to serve the Lord and be in His presence. They as well need a season of refreshment, so we come together once a year.

The topic of our week was well - I want to save that for the end of the testimony. You see, each year a team of organizers and participants set out to design the weekend around a specific need they had prayed about over the previous year and all activities, talks and events around that "theme" would take on that shape. More on that later.

The time together with our friends went as planned although this year I just could not sit alone with God very comfortably. I wasn't sure if it was a spiritual stirring or a physical manifestation of some sort trying to reveal itself to me. When I say physical, we do commune (eat) quite well together for three days so as the doctors would say maybe just a little backed up in the plumbing department, so in a sense I am referring to the condition of my health. I just was not feeling well like I usually do, and I wasn't really able to pinpoint a particular problem. I chalked it off as just being away from home, maybe a little tired and not resting well in my own bed. After all it was still this amazing weekend filled with great messages, encouraging friends and an environment that looked as if it was brush stroked by

God just for our enjoyment (a mountain top experience despite my health issues).

As the anointed weekend wrapped up and tears of departure and promises of continued relations were confirmed with our close brothers we said our good-byes. It was time to make the trek back to the Midwest. A six-hundred mile excursion that left plenty of room for more intimate follow-up conversation among the few that journeyed out that year with me; carpooling with 3 grown men- that could have been the source of discomfort.

I started the first leg of the trip home only to make it to the Pennsylvania border, which I would estimate to be about one hundred miles. I was unable to get comfortable in the seat regardless of position and a pain had begun to take over my lower extremities to the point that I was forced to stretch out. I was hoping to contribute a share of driving later the next morning.

The next several hours consisted of some ibuprofen- which my body doesn't care for since a bleeding ulcer revealed itself years prior- and me curled up in the fetal position with a makeshift pillow, moaning at every exit ramp and sway of the vehicle.

What was this that was happening? An anointed weekend and I go home constipated, or with kidneys stones or maybe something crazier like my kidneys falling out? "Oh, thanks, Lord... I got this..." Thankfully, I was able to sleep, interrupted of course. I spent my time drowsing on and off and intermittently peering through glazed eyes at the blur of highway signs and overhead highway messages flying past the window at seventy-some miles per hour. It gave me a small sense of our progress while I moaned in discomfort. The trip finally landed us back at the parking lot of our home church. It was about 6 AM according to the voice coming across the radio and the morning light was cutting through a brilliant neon sky. The air had that refreshing crispness of an early autumn morning, another reminder that the fragrance of God was still very close. All of this was very pleasing; what wasn't so pleasing was the movement necessary to reposition myself outside of the vehicle for goodbyes to travel companions who were precious enough to allow me to rest (probably cracking jokes the whole way too but hey, that's ok we're friends.)

Within moments the general pain I had experienced throughout the trip targeted itself under my lower right rib cage invoking tremendous dry heaves of pain, sounds that would overtake the orchestra of birds chirping much the same as a trombone would belt out a base line over the gentle trilling of flutes. It was a harmony of sound I didn't find too pleasant. Immediately I asked my partner in Christian crime to rush me to the hospital which was about fifteen minutes from our location, because something was not right! Every cough, every significant intake of fresh air would send shards of pain down my right-side rib cage. A very unfamiliar experience to me, but a necessary one and, might I add, timed perfectly. Within several minutes we rounded the corner into the ER drive and I exited with a bit of relief knowing answers may be minutes away especially at 6 AM when the ER department was practically at a crawl though certainly anticipating the day's rush of medical mishaps.

The typical protocols leading up to information was exchanged and a series of tests initiated. I turned to my minister friend who drove me there and who was graciously sitting with me trying to stay awake and said, "Here we go!"

I sent my brother in Christ home after such a long night, (yes I was kicking him out, nothing he could do anyway at this point) and my wife was on the way up to take relief. Good or bad results to be determined at this point.

I began my Christian checklist.

Indestructible -check

Impenetrable -check

Godly -check

Faithful - check

Solid – check

Unwavering – check

Christian - check

Demeanor - check

25

I thought I had it covered until the attending returned with some details that would alter my future. "Hello, Mr. Catron, may I come in?"... "Yes, please feel free...give it to me straight doctor. It's all good. What's up? Did I eat too much...?"

Humor - check

Confidence - check

(Sorry, forgot a few there.)

"No, sir, we observed, on the CT scan performed a little bit ago, some lesions on your pancreas and your right lung is elevated..."

"Say what, Doctor? That's CATRON correct...? Check the room number out there, did ya?"

"Yes, sir."

After a few moments, "Okay, what does all that mean?"

The doctor then said, "Has there been any signs of cancer in your family or your own history?"

Okay, at this point I'm looking up at this beautiful image airbrushed or painted onto a fluorescent light cover (I suppose it was one of those ceiling tiles designed to help patients remain calm and relaxed during moments like these) and think, "God, you laid that out for the world to gaze upon its beauty and I get lesions?"

I manage to keep that Pastoral image of strength and "God's got this!" persona until I am able to break free for a moment which at that point meant turning over to my side. After all, it was just constipation not cancer, what in the world?! I suppose I still wasn't sure I heard the word cancer correctly. *Cancer?* What a crazy whirlwind of emotions were transpiring right then. Calls would have to be made; biopsies and tests would need to be done, on and on and on. "Ain't nobody got time for that!" (A YouTube spiff recently watched that made me laugh.) Because I had a mentality that nothing slows me down except a casket and my head hitting the hinge upon entry.

Then I remembered the theme of the weekend I had just participated in, (I told you I would share it with you later) "Being broken and following someone with a limp."

Wow, God. What just happened? If all this plays out (and the following weeks would to one degree be a blessing since it was not the pancreas but the colon and the liver that were stage IV riddled with cancer), I am broken, truly broken in the physical sense, and soon after would reveal the spiritual sense too.

My wife and I had a lot of tears together and a lot of time to talk about what just went down in the emergency room. She has truly been a blessing to me from God. She walks by my side through every storm and valley and supports me unconditionally. Thank you, dear!

Here we go, what am I willing to do with it? Being broken, the cancer, the fight, the ministry, my life? After a very brief emotional transition period, one morning I was standing in the shower and I cried out to God: "Okay, God, I must become less so that you can become more. I am broken. Allow people to see you through me and I will be the limper of the following."

Unless you have been to war you can't speak on its behalf, unless you have been to the spiritual battlefield, you have no credibility. John says:

"He must become greater; I must
become less" John 3:30 NKJV

John says this as a reminder that He ministers through us, we do not minister through Him.

Truth no.1: I have been broken. Mine is a physical one.

Truth no.2: I will be used by God in all my emptiness to fill His needs through me.

Truth no.3: It isn't about me. In my weakness, Apostle Paul says His strength is made perfect.

Truth no. 4: ALL things work together for good. Not my good And I believe it should state, "For His Glory all things should work together for those called to His purpose."

Truth no. 5: I had no idea what was going to transpire.

Truth no.6: I would become a daily encouragement to so many that would cross my path in the following months and years.

Truth no. 7: I would motivate people into deeper relationships with Christ just because of the trust they observed in me.

Truth no. 8: I would be the hands and feet of Jesus regardless of what happened on my cancer journey, because I gave it all to Him that morning in the shower. There was nothing left to accept responsibility for.

Truth no. 9: I would acknowledge I was His child.

Truth no. 10: I would acknowledge it was not my ministry but His to Glorify.

In the following months, approximately fifteen chemo sessions and various other interventions, a lot of prayer intervention, crying, laughing and sharing this testimony, God would move me from plastered with tumors to remission in four months. To date the cancer has returned, only to rear its ugly head back in my liver some. So, the battle rages on. I believe the chemo rounds are up in the fifties now with different treatments and medicines being applied. This is due to detrimental neuropathy setting in and almost being irreversible and other side effects causing irreversible harm if the treatment regimen continued as planned. Fortunately, there were other treatment plans to try but all carried similar if not more irritating side effects, hair loss, nausea, skin irritations, finger nail loss etc.

Until recently the battle was cancer, which changed just before the time of the writing of this book, March of 2019, which also prompted the writing of this book. While visiting Maryland, God revealed a pounding in my chest that would be the workings of a widow maker heart attack in the LAD portion of the heart, with 100% blockage. Don't ask me what LAD is (actually I just WebMD searched it for ya!). LAD means the left anterior descending, the main part of the heart that does like 70% of the pumping. There is not that much alphabet beyond my name (just a pastor, remember) so that's all the knowledge I have for you. Within twenty minutes of identifying the heart attack and getting transportation, I was yet again in the hospital, this time for my heart. Within an hour and a half from symptom start, I was recovering from a double stent Cath lab trip, instead of lying on a slab in the morgue. The faithful Father had protected me once again.

I was still broken, broken even more now that my heart was only pumping at 39%- half the rate of a healthier, younger model. God walked all over me that day with His protection. A Promise He would never leave me nor forsake me and that is why I follow a faithful God. Not so that I can live longer, but because He promises to let me live as long as I may be able to- through spirit or body- serve others of His needs for them. I love you God!

So my testimony ends there for now. All walks of my life from abusive bully of an immature young adult filled with irresponsible behaviors, to God centered, God focused, God, God, God. Everything that I am; broken enough to allow Him to use me in any way He chooses. Whether it be in the trenches, on the other side of the hospital bedrails sitting with dying patients, my own family needs, my community, the pulpit, the pews and even the side of my bed at night. I seek Him continuously through every facet of my life because I know what He is capable of doing for me and to me. Who said, "That's my story and I'm sticking to it?" That's it. That's my story. I thank you for your prayerfully receiving this into your heart and I pray it becomes motivation for you to explore your own testimony soon, if you have not already, simply to see how God is using and molding you to be used for His glory as well. God bless you!

6

SELF-CRITIQUE, ASSESSMENT & HEART TO HEARTS

S O HERE WE ARE, AT AN HONEST POINT IN OUR RELATIONSHIP BETWEEN the Creator and ourselves. After all, He knew you before you were conceived. He probably has a pretty good idea of who you are now, right? Be Honest. Adam was hiding in the cool night breeze after committing his sins with Eve. (Genesis 3:9 not published, but referenced) When God came strolling through the garden asking Adam "Where are you?" it wasn't a physical location God was inquiring about, it was where Adam's heart was. God was expecting confirmation of what He already knew. (Some denominations call that confession.) Adam's heart was far from God at the moment, lost in the forbidden fruit at the center of the Garden.

We use the term Omnipresent as a character of God: omni meaning one and present meaning well, the obvious. God is ever present at the same time, all the time and that's everywhere. Why does God care about His child's heart? It's simple; God is a God of love. His plan for us was only the best before the fall in the garden occurred. It is the beginning of our story of salvation and the need for Jesus.

God asks us, just as He asked Adam, "Where are you?" And the question each of us must honestly answer to God is exactly what He already knows, (remember, He's God, after all) your emotional GPS. Your emotional GPS, what in the world is that? Interestingly, it's a way to question how close or far you are from God. Where is your heart in relationship to connecting with God? He knows your heart already, so what this truly becomes is a moment of soul searching, He wants *you* to find out where you are, regardless of what He already knows.

A big part of a relationship with the Lord is soul searching, a process of figuring out what is most important to you. Soul searching often leads to ministry opportunities we never thought possible. One of the scariest things to look at, beyond a good Stephen King novel, or a Wes Craven movie, is your soul. There is so much hidden in there waiting to be discovered. There are stories from our past and present that make up who we are and why we behave the way we do. There are good and bad memories which curve our thought processes as well. God just wants you to know you so that you can better serve Him. Perhaps the easiest way to state it is, your emotional GPS is the location of your heart in relationship with your life. Where are you in your love for God? Are you nearing towards Him daily, are you stagnant, are you running towards Him eagerly anticipating what He has in store for you? As long as you are not plotting against Him, moving away from Him, He will be content. Don't ignore Him; He certainly doesn't care for that too much. There was hardly a Jewish Zealot in existence willing to put *that* much on the line, so God, in this author's opinion, doesn't expect an "all in" at first mentality. Some may differ with that opinion, but He also loved His doubting disciples just as much as His more ambitious ones. God does understand the human far more then we give Him credit for. We are doubting creatures in our nature. We have all treaded in the waters of doubt, is this really for me, or not? Can I do this, or not?

The need for self-critique and evaluation is important to help determine how you can best serve Him with the predisposition you currently carry. In other words, are you outgoing, love people and love watching them grow and blossom into true God seekers? Are you comfortable seeing people thrive and flourish past your own abilities? Are you an introvert? Aggressive in nature, quiet, listening, empathetic? Do you cry with others? Are you able to feel their emotions and able to reflect with them empathetically? Are you a teacher, do you receive bits of knowledge from nowhere for someone else's benefit? Do you feel a deep desire for people to know the truth that will keep them from eternity in Hell (411- I hope this is always a yes!!)?

Digging a little deeper now, there are a ton of internet services you can use to analyze information about yourself through a series of simple questionnaire type responses; these are called spiritual inventories. Even spiritual gift inventories exist, and leadership style inventories exist. These types of audits, if you will, are highly beneficial in preventing you from going down an exploratory rabbit hole only to find out you don't like carrots at all. The cost is often free, or minimal, and you get a more in-depth report of yourself than you would probably be comfortable with acknowledging.

On the other end of the spectrum, there are resources at a more professional level, requiring interviews and significant financial investments to aid in your understanding of self; these are through programs such as Pastoral Education. Perhaps this is not something of great concern at this point, but I mention it now so that you become aware of what is available. Clinical Pastoral Education sessions or internship programs are usually held at local hospitals and provide intern type positions to help grow an individual into a place of ministry understanding and how a person might fit into that mix. Ministry can be a complex place where the heart meets the mind, meets the soul and the spirit. Adding to the complexity of ministry is your subject or person you are interacting with, blending all these pieces together you begin to form your full ministry experience.

Take some time in this area, really tuning in to who you are and the whys of you being there. Let God speak to you, let friends talk things out, and let professionals explore ministry with you from multiple perspectives. If your interest in ministry remains strong, you will find great value in knowing who you are before entering ministry and perhaps a good sense (discernment) of where your passions lay waiting.

WHERE DOES YOUR PASSION LAY?

T HIS ISN'T A DIFFICULT CHAPTER TO WALK THROUGH. THE QUESTION ASKS you, what motivates your ministry efforts?

"I, therefore, the prisoner of the Lord, beseech you to walk worthy of the calling with which you were called, with all lowliness and gentleness, with longsuffering, bearing with one another in love, endeavoring to keep the unity of the Spirit in the bond of peace. There is one body and one Spirit" Ephesians 4:1-4 NKJV

"And He Himself gave some to be apostles, some prophets, some evangelists, and some pastors and teachers, for the equipping of the saints for the work of ministry, for the edifying of the body of Christ," Ephesians 4:11-12 NKJV

We all have roles in His kingdom, and we all have our own unique abilities, known as gifts, to fill certain roles he has established. Where your honesty concludes from the last chapter can help. Are you able to get a better sense of where God wants you to be in His kingdom? Where He wants you to serve Him? One that edifies the body (there is that word again, the 'lifting up' or caring for of a person in some capacity.) Burnout and frustration begin to occur when you don't give yourself the credit for what you can accomplish and try to accomplish tasks that you're just not equipped to handle. Now this doesn't mean God doesn't get the glory. This simply means encouragement, acknowledging you're doing everything for God's glory. Edifying the body to maximize the ability to serve the King! Okay, if you still haven't figured it out yet, it's called taking care of yourself!

Did life throw you a curve ball like it did me with my trials in cancer and heart issues? There is an age-old question asked by millions of people who question the existence of God around them. Why do bad things happen to good people? The truth is good and bad can happen to anybody and I consider myself an anybody. If I didn't serve a loving God, I would be looking at serving a vengeful God and I don't for one minute believe that could be possible. So why my health concerns? Because God is able to use them just as if He wrote me a check for a million dollars and took all my worries away. He could use it for His Glory, because I am willing to be used.

Did I mention I have never been the greatest orator, quickest reader, or most sophisticated entertainer? But I do have a deep desire to counsel and listen to people that are in crisis situations. Families grieving and facing death sparks my passion to help bring peace and comfort into their lives. Just as much passion, perhaps, as I feel when I am behind the pulpit sharing the truth that sets people free. I am not a great street evangelist, but I know ministers that knock it out of the park with that style of ministry. So please take some time to look at your life, your style, your personality, and formulate some thoughts about what motivated you to become a pastor in the first place. You may have had an experience that connects you with a specific opportunity in ministry, one that you are not even aware of yet.

Wise warning: don't fall into the prestige, glamor and stardom that come to a ½ percent of the population seeking to draw a relativist crowd or chauffer a level of entertainment value for the sake of the Gospel. Remember, if you want to be a minister, the Gospel only needs someone to speak it or share it through action. No amount of smoke, mirrors, or sound quality can change the effectiveness of the message being delivered. People needing the Gospel will hear the Gospel when the Holy Spirit falls upon them.

IDENTIFY THE HELP

B EFORE WE IDENTIFY HELP, LET US TAKE A MOMENT TO DEFINE IT. HELP should be considered an influential source that provides godly wisdom directing you always towards the path of the cross. Everything a minister can accomplish is solely due to the cross. It has the fuel that fills a pastor's soul. It becomes a motivation that ignites every conversation. A friend can be a source of help if they are of godly value, a trusted Pastor, Deacon, Elder or even Layperson can be a valuable source given their background and desire to center around the cross. Everything serves a purpose of godliness and should be gauged and measured off the alignment with the cross.

If the cross does not hold significance in your judgement at this point, please consider discussing the value of the cross in ministry with a trusted minister. The cross is what frees us from bondage; the cross is what restores humanity to God. The cross is the answer to a sinful nature, and it is the only way to land in Heaven with God. The cross was "Thy Will" for Jesus, (see The Lord's Prayer Matthew 6:10) and He fulfilled it with obedience. The significance of the cross can be compared to the scales of justice, in that everything a pastor holds near and dear to them weighs in comparison.

I will lift up my eyes to the hills—
From whence comes my help?

My help comes from the Lord,
Who made heaven and earth.
Psalm 121:1-2 NKJV

The cross becomes the crux of eternal life in the face of eternity in two very distinct locations. In other words, it's life or death of the soul. How much value are you willing to place on the credibility of your help when it comes to a crucial matter such as someone about to take their last breath? The burden of this eternal decision over someone's spiritual life should be a powerful influence in your desire to serve the Lord with all the right tools and resources possible. It is an eternal decision available to us until we take that last breath, to accept Jesus Christ as our personal Savior or to not accept Him.

"But seek first the kingdom of God and His
righteousness, and all these things shall be
added to you." Matthew 6:33 NKJV

There may be no greater help than help that is always grounded in the truth of scripture. Scripture provides its own truth and should never be reversed, we should never intend on reading a scripture and applying our truth to it; not how it works. There is plenty of scripture in the Holy text that we can seem to apply this process to, but don't. For example, many people quote the Bible as saying, "God will never give you more than you can handle." Not true. (Survey says "0" or big red X if we are playing Family Feud.) The Bible does say things like, "I will never leave you nor forsake you," Hebrews 13:5 NKJV, or cleanliness is next to godliness, when the Lord sought favor over the needy and poor (those that tended to their spiritual need's versus physical needs-I would go so far as to say He cares more about the cleanliness of our inner soul). So, be careful when using the weapons of the Bible, used wrongly (intentional or not) it will kill your credibility and serve you no true purpose other than the potential of ministering someone *out* of heaven.

The Bible clearly and explicitly talks about sin. In Romans 1:18 the Bible talks about God's wrath on sin:

> For the wrath of God is revealed from heaven
> against all ungodliness and unrighteousness
> of men, who suppress the truth in
> unrighteousness, Romans 1:18 NKJV
> (Further along)
> Therefore God also gave them up to uncleanness,
> in the lusts of their hearts, to dishonor their
> bodies among themselves, who exchanged the
> truth of God for the lie, and worshiped and
> served the creature rather than the Creator, who
> is blessed forever. Amen. Romans 1:24-25 NKJV

There is more in that section of scripture about God turning you over to your practices. He will 'Know you no more.' Really? Does it say that? Sure does. I don't have a Master's degree in Theological studies, but God sure revealed that to me through those passages. Regardless, God is fair. He gives us a choice and we are free to make the choice, and with every choice there is a consequence.

Don't merely tell others that God's grace will continue to cover them if you don't believe a true heart transplant is necessary. The disciples say, "Confess with your mouth Jesus is Lord and you will be saved," but we better start looking closer at what a saved person is still doing in the bar at all hours of the night or cheating on their spouse.

Chances are they didn't hear everything God was speaking to them during that confession of faith.

Truth, truth, truth, I don't want anything else on my consciousness when someone is standing before the throne. There is power in the name of Jesus and if that is true, there is power in every aspect of Jesus: His life, His words, His ministry and especially His destination.

What else comes to mind when we think of help? There is not a single Pastor that will tell you that their help is not grounded in prayer. Fervent, honest, "Lord, I cannot do this without you," prayer. You know, Prayer is not as difficult as many make it out to be. (After all, such an agonizing task to talk to God; the pressure, the pressure it's insurmountable!) Telling God everything God already knows may seem like it falls into the department of redundancy, but God truly delights in hearing from His children. After all, how much heavenly trumpeted choir music can one God listen to?

"Ask, and it will be given to you; seek, and
you will find; knock, and it will be opened
to you. For everyone who asks receives, and
he who seeks finds, and to him who knocks
it will be opened." Matthew 7:7-9 NKJV

Psalm 46:10 says, "Be still and know that I am God"

Whoa, what more help can come to someone that meditates and practices on that? The Lord is saying in all circumstances to us, "Be still, and have the confidence that I am God." Trust that whatever this season, or moment, is in your life, I am in complete control over it.

I cannot reiterate enough that to use all those tools means that you need to have complete confidence in the truth behind them, and the only way to accomplish that is to spend time with Him in all the different capacities possible. Quiet time, prayer time, reading and learning about Him time, fellowship with others time, time spent much the same as you would when learning about someone new in your own physical life relationship. There is no difference between developing a relationship with God than any other being. Well, there is one: He will never fail you.

9

MOVING FORWARD
(THAT BOAT THING)

S O, WE HAVE COME TO THE PLACE (HOPEFULLY OVER SOME SERIOUS
reflection, prayer, and crying) before the Lord that you are ready
to take some sort of step. This is where I draw you to the boat
story. The story you may know; the application may seem new to you.
It is one revelation of this passage that should be significant in any
walk of life.

"Immediately Jesus made His disciples get into the
boat and go before Him to the other side, while He
sent the multitudes away. And when He had sent the
multitudes away, He went up on the mountain by
Himself to pray. Now when evening came, He was
alone there. But the boat was now in the middle of the
sea, tossed by the waves, for the wind was contrary.
Now in the fourth watch of the night Jesus went to
them, walking on the sea. And when the disciples
saw Him walking on the sea, they were troubled,
saying, "It is a ghost!" And they cried out for fear. But
immediately Jesus spoke to them, saying, "Be of good
cheer! It is I; do not be afraid." And Peter answered
Him and said, "Lord, if it is You, command me to

come to You on the water." So, He said, "Come." And when Peter had come down out of the boat, he walked on the water to go to Jesus. But when he saw that the wind was boisterous, he was afraid; and beginning to sink he cried out, saying, "Lord, save me!" And immediately Jesus stretched out His hand and caught him, and said to him, "O you of little faith, why did you doubt?" And when they got into the boat, the wind ceased. Then those who were in the boat came and worshiped Him, saying, "Truly You are the Son of God.""" Matt 14:22-33 NKJV

Take a few minutes together with the Lord and read this through; it should become clear by the end of our chapter how significant this passage of scripture is, not only to ministry, but all aspects of our life.

Jesus had just spent a great deal of energy ministering to the community on the hillsides of the Sea of Galilee. He was tired and sent His disciples off in the boat only to catch up with them following a little alone time with Dad (God). He prayed and rested, prayed and rested, and then decided to join His disciples that had already launched into the sea. Because He was God, He walked across the water to catch up with them instead of waiting for the next water taxi to cruise by. The sea water was a bit busy from the storms brewing around the area, not uncommon in that region for a sudden gust of a storm to arise. The Disciples saw something approaching and called out in fear, thinking that some sort of apparition or ghost was approaching from the sea. Jesus assured them that it was just Him and things seem to settle, except in Peter's heart. Peter was so anxious to see Jesus, that He asked Jesus to join Him in the water, (as if there was a tiki bar or somewhere they could sit and share some lemonade). Not sure what Peter was thinking at this point, other than he wanted to be with Jesus no matter the cost.) So, Jesus invited Peter into the water and Peter began to realize the environment he had just entered was stormy and scary, and perhaps a little dangerous and unsafe, and began to sink. Peter cried out to Jesus to save him and immediately Jesus responded with an outreached hand, grabbing Him from the waters to safety.

As we reflect on this story and apply it to any part of our life, it will reveal again the centrality of the cross in our lives and what Jesus, our Lord has done. Please don't take the injection of my humor into the story as any means of lessening or devaluing its purpose. It is truly one of my own personal life passages / verses that I cling to in times of trouble.

God responds. We act and the Son of man responds with urgency (immediately reaching down). Stepping out of the boat and into the trusting arms of Jesus- that is what this passage is about. You are either just beginning or are considering the tremendous honor of ministry, serving the Lord with your life. We want it so desperately that often it is done without looking around or considering our personal investment. When we look at the surroundings- the storm, the land, the safety net of our comfort zone- we are not looking at Jesus. If you have made the leap already into ministry you, at this point, should be solely focused on Jesus. Looking back to those safety nets will cause us to reflect on our limitations and we will sink. We will find ourselves having to call out to Jesus in that moment to save us from ourselves (our safety nets.) We want to be with Jesus so badly that we make the ultimate decision to follow Him and follow Him completely- that is what this is all about. Stepping out of the boat to be with Him and do what He is doing. So, we are in the water and what happens? Do we also sink? Do we plummet to the depths of the sea, or does Jesus reach out to us and save us?

Why does this happen in the first place? I keep saying being centered on the cross, but what does that truly mean? If you are centered and focused on Jesus, you don't see storms, you don't observe insurmountable obstacles; you don't see doubt, worry, or anxiety. In fact, if we are centered (focused) on Jesus, we cannot even see the shoreline that provides your typical comforts of safety (if you can swim that is). We see nothing but Jesus, Jesus, Jesus. He is what I would choose to see first thing in the morning and last thing at night as the sun burrows into the west.

"I can do all things through Christ who strengthens me." Philippians 4:13 NKJV

Perhaps this is a familiar passage of scripture, if not I hope it will be to you soon. It speaks of what God is capable of doing through you. There's a catch: faith. Let's throw another one out there for you to absorb.

"Now faith is the substance of things hoped for, the evidence of things not seen." Hebrews 11:1 NKJV

Wait, what? Yes, the Biblical definition of faith. You can't see it; you must trust it (GOD) is there for you in all circumstances. There is plenty of evidence of that truth. Simply go back to my testimony, if you're in question. Evidence does not have to be earth-shattering; it can be the simplest of proofs. So faith: keeping our eyes off the environment (everything that is going on and meant to cause a distraction), will keep us walking on the water towards Jesus. Become unfocused, look at the familiar, the safe, the shore line, and it suddenly isn't about Jesus anymore, it's about you. Try if you might, but I'll take my chances with the King first.

That's it, that's how you move forward. Place every ounce of trust in Jesus and if you begin to falter or take your eyes off Him, cry out to Him, and He will immediately reach a hand down and pull you to safety. Let's not repeat where safety is (it isn't the shoreline). Work hard, remain honest and full of integrity, and lastly for this chapter, I will throw in having the mindset of Christ Jesus. Let's look:

"Therefore, if there is any consolation in Christ, if any comfort of love, if any fellowship of the Spirit, if any affection and mercy, fulfill my joy by being like-minded, having the same love, being of one accord, of one mind. Let nothing be done through selfish ambition or conceit, but in lowliness of mind let each esteem others better than himself. Let each of you look out not only for his own interests, but also for the interests of others. Let this mind be in you which was also in Christ Jesus, who, being in the form of God, did not consider it robbery to be equal with God, but made Himself of no reputation, taking the form of a bondservant, and coming in the likeness of men. And being found in appearance as a man, He humbled Himself and became obedient to the point of death, even the death of the cross." Philippians 2:1-8 NKJV

In case you or I forgot, which I do often and need reminded, the Gospel is an instruction manual for life. Take advantage of it.

Recap: in ministry, as it should be in life also, Jesus is our focus. Regardless of what is around us, Jesus should always remain our focus. This is called being cross centered, in my opinion. Jesus's sole purpose in life was obedience to the Father and His obedience was the cross, to be the perfect sacrifice for our sins so that we could be re-established (sanctified) as God's children. Because of Jesus's obedience we have that ability now to get right with God. Jesus centered ministry and Jesus centered life means your obedience is following His path to the cross and not wavering from it. We see waves crashing down on us and will need the saving hand of Jesus to bring us back into focus. Looking, focusing, thinking about anything other than Jesus will cause that to happen. So keep your eyes off the familiar, the shoreline, the safety net; stay in the storm and focus, focus, focus on those beautiful eyes of Christ. He will never leave you, nor forsake you (for fish food). He will weather every storm you remain focused on Him through, and together a new glorious victory will be observed, one soul at a time. Satan won't be happy. The storm may get rougher and the shoreline further away to the point it becomes a thin braid separating the heavens from the earth. Which, I remind you, the shoreline is still the same size; it's just your view that has changed. But Jesus, now Jesus, no matter where you observe Him from, will never change in appearance, attraction, size, shape or meaning. Whether you just stepped out of the boat or are being held in His arms; He is unwavering in capacity.

Step out of the boat, in complete trust, and He will guide your ministry to accomplish His Glory. Matthew 28 is the great commission to, "Go into all nations preaching the Gospel."

Go,

Gospel,

Good News,

God . . .

All start with the letters "G & O"

G_{et} O_{ut} of the boat and

G_{et} O_{n}

with your purpose to serve the Lord.

There is no greater honor than to serve a King who died for you so that you may live with Him in eternity. Don't you want that opportunity for others as well? Maybe this is where you head back to the book store for a friend to get another copy to study together. Pray for God to speak to you through this journey. Keep praying urgently. Put a pot of coffee on, or one of those energy drinks, (if your heart is healthy enough for those products) and power through a great evening of talking and listening to God, your Abba, Dad. He loves you.

10

EDUCATIONAL BENEFITS

C HANGING YOUR LIFE INTO A LIFE OF MINISTRY CAN HAVE ITS BENEFITS. One of those benefits is being able to work alongside passionate caregivers in a variety of settings that are ministering in ways you may not even recognize as being of Christ. As I had mentioned earlier, I had the distinct honor and privilege to be welcomed into families' homes in some of the most vulnerable times there are. Jesus Himself was called to the bedside of many who lay sick and faced death. Having been called to the tomb of Lazarus after Lazarus had been deceased three days, Jesus revealed compassion through the shortest verse written in the Bible and it simply states that "Jesus Wept." John 11:35 NKJV

It is a model of Christ to weep with friends and loved ones going through the process of loss of life. To a minister, working with grieving families is not new, but to a new minister, grief can be a strange environment to encounter at first. It comes fully charged with an onslaught and variety of emotions and requires some skills, training and education can oftentimes assist. That was partly me; the life of a Hospice Chaplain. I was told in training it would probably take a good eighteen months to see just about all I would see and even then, new things would spring up on occasion. That's about right.

There are a variety of educational paths a minister of any caliber can access from universities: studies in theology, Biblical history, doctrines and apologetics, even counseling and more common worldly needs. None the less, it requires cracking open the books. So, if you desire to go through seminary and receive your master's, you will find at the other end employment options can greatly increase. Options such as the medical industry, civil services or military services, law enforcement, sports and even some church denominations require a strict degree before ordination. Just remember, education comes with several price tags, beyond the dollars and cents of book fees and semester credit fees. They require your time; time possibly away from your family or your ministry efforts. Make every effort to figure things out early and investigate what educational approach will work best for your scenario. Hospitals oftentimes offer Clinical Pastoral Education opportunities, but residency's in CPE require a master's degree to be accepted, while internships are solely short-term based learning opportunities offering the same benefits under extended multiple registration processes. CPE also provides invaluable resources into oneself, teaching and helping you discover how you think, feel and react in environments you may work within. Most hospital websites will provide resources to information if they are available through their network.

Other opportunities include shadowing and simply working the streets to learn the ropes through real world experiences, which we all can say with a level of certainty, is irreplaceable and invaluable.

11

WHY A MINISTER?
THE HARD ROAD

Then He said to *them* all, "If anyone desires to come after Me, let him deny himself, and take up his cross daily, and follow Me. For whoever desires to save his life will lose it, but whoever loses his life for My sake will save it. For what profit is it to a man if he gains the whole world, and is himself destroyed or lost? Luke 9:23-25 NKJV

MINISTRY IS NOT FOR THE LIGHT HEARTED, IT OFTEN TAKES THICK skin, loneliness, isolation, dedication no matter what the outcome, and a serious thinker mentality. We are called into the darkest of places.

For everyone practicing evil hates the light and does not come to the light, lest his deeds should be exposed. But he who does the truth comes to the light, that his

deeds may be clearly seen, that they have been done in God." John 3:20-21 NKJV

Yes, think about this, this is two-thousand year old plus scripture that is very applicable today. In the veil of darkness evil is practiced. Nightclubs, back alleys, after hours scenes, murders typically occur at night (although lately that course has changed), adultery; if you want to get extreme, even restaurants and movie theaters turn down their lights. Ok, I know we may be pushing those facets a bit, but you get the point. This is where the minister is called to be effective. Jesus met people where they were, He did not wait around for those in need to come to Him. So, we work often in darkness. Among the darkness lies a deeper darkness called the spiritual realm where principalities of all types are free to roam and wreak havoc where possible. What better target than to attack the ones that pose the biggest threat to the prince of this world, Satan? Yes, that would be you and I, the ones equipped with scripture and knowledge, ready to go to war at a moment's notice for those that are lost, leaving ourselves susceptible and vulnerable to attacks.

I have been in situations where the enemy was spiritually at large and left with nausea and migraines on more than one occasion. I have had to pull over to the side of the road in fear of passing out. I have preached on Sunday mornings behind the pulpit to go home crying, tired and exhausted for the next two days. Must have been a good sermon! The point is, we are walking down dark roads, sometimes ill-equipped, oftentimes not, but we are still making the trip, and we are the ones putting ourselves out there for the sake of the great commission and to spread God's eternal love to all the nations. What better cause? There isn't one. That is why we claim our coffins sliding head first screaming, "What a ride!"

Why a minister? The answer: because there is no greater honor than to lay down one's life for another's. The Apostle Paul was torn between going to be with Jesus and serving Jesus here. Are you torn? Is there that much passion in you to calm the storms and straighten paths for those that are weak and ill-equipped? I promise you would not have to go outside of a one-half mile radius of where you stand at this very moment to find someone in need.

Do yourself the favor, find someone to minister-to-the-minster right now, before you even get started, because I promise you, you are already under attack just for raising the thought of entering ministry. You need somebody right now that will be praying for you. I, myself, (once the ink has dried on this book), will have begun the process of praying for each of you that opens and closes each chapter of this book.

If I may go back to the beginning of this chapter, highlighting the scripture from Luke 9: Jesus tells us to pick up your cross daily. This is glorious news from above. Because of the word 'your' it then becomes a customized cross that He has provided you on your journey and He promises that when you pick it up, you will be able to see it through. The cross you carry may contain a different burden every day for you, but it is your part of the process, your strength of the church, your responsibility, and it is customized for you. At that point we deny ourselves and we center on the cross, so as to not sink, and we go and we do what is called of us to do: "To be the light of the world." We go where is light needed the most: in the darkest of places, flushing out the evil lurking within. Good luck, you got this. That's why you're going to be a minister!

12

SCRIPTURES TO KNOW
BEFORE YOU GO

I T IS IMPORTANT TO MENTION BEFORE BEGINNING THIS CHAPTER, THAT although this book is not meant to be an intimidating source of doctrine and theological beliefs, we must be astutely aware of the sincerity of this endeavor. It is not to be approached lightly; you ultimately will be held accountable for a number of souls that you may decide to shepherd into eternity.

The Bible speaks clearly of the qualifications of a pastor so let's take a look.

Remember this scripture is entitled, "Qualities of an Elder." But as a Pastor, we are held above reproach, so we must be qualified at any level of the church to be the shepherd.

"For this reason I left you in Crete, that you should set in order the things that are lacking, and appoint elders in every city as I commanded you— if a man is blameless, the husband of one wife, having faithful children not accused of dissipation or insubordination. For a bishop must be blameless, as a steward of God, not self-willed, not quick-tempered, not given to wine, not violent, not greedy for money, but hospitable, a lover of what is good, sober-minded, just, holy, self-controlled, holding fast the faithful word as he has been taught, that he may be able, by sound doctrine, both to exhort and convict those who contradict." Titus 1:5-9

1. A pastor must be devoted to his wife (Titus 1:6; 1 Tim 3:2). The pastor's marriage should imitate Christ's love for His church—His bride (Eph. 5:22 ff.). A Pastor must love his wife all inclusively.

2. A pastor's children must be in submission. We typically hear of the terrors of the 'Preacher's Kids' (Titus 1:6; 1 Tim 3:4-5). It becomes about being responsible and in charge of his home.

3. A pastor is a faithful steward (Titus 1:7), a manager of God's resources and Jesus's flock.

4. A pastor must be humble and gentle.

*At this point in lieu of space consumption please continue this study with Titus 1. Your home must be in order before you should attempt God's home management.

Scripture to meditate on during your transformation process into ministry:

"Therefore, my beloved brethren, be steadfast, immovable, always abounding in the work of the Lord, knowing that your labor is not in vain in the Lord." 1 Corinthians 15:58 NKJV

"And let us not grow weary while doing good, for in due season we shall reap if we do not lose heart." Galatians 6:9 NKJV

"And my God shall supply all your need according to His riches in glory by Christ Jesus." Philippians 4:19 NKJV

"My brethren, let not many of you become teachers, knowing that we shall receive a stricter judgment." James 3:1 NKJV

"For God so loved the world that He gave His only begotten Son, that whoever believes in Him should not perish but have everlasting life. 17 For God did not send His Son into the world to condemn the world, but that the world through Him might be saved." John 3:16-17 NKJV

"Humble yourselves in the sight of the Lord,
and He will lift you up." James 4:10 NKJV

"He must increase, but I must
decrease." John 3:30 NKJV

"I can do all things through Christ who
strengthens me." Philippians 4:13 NKJV

"Trust in the Lord with all your heart,
And lean not on your own understanding;
In all your ways acknowledge Him,
And He shall direct your paths."
Proverbs 3:5-6 NKJV

"but we will give ourselves continually to prayer and to the
ministry of the word."

Acts 6:4 NKJV
Best two for last but certainly not
an all-inclusive listing.

The Great Commandment

Jesus said to him, 'You shall love the Lord your God with all your heart, with all your soul, and with all your mind.' This is the first and great commandment. And the second is like it: 'You shall love your neighbor as yourself.' On these two commandments hang all the Law and the Prophets." Matthew 22:37-40

The Great Commission

"And Jesus came and spoke to them "All authority has been given to Me in heaven and on earth. Go therefore and make disciples of all the nations, baptizing them in the name of the Father and of the Son and of the Holy Spirit, teaching them to observe all things that I have commanded you; and lo, I am with you always, even to the end of the age." Amen. Matthew 28:18-20 NKJV

Journal of my own important scriptures here.

- _____

- _____

- _____

- _____

- _____

- _____

- _____

- _____

- _____

- _____

- _____

- _____

- _____

-
-
-
-
-
-
-

My prayer is every page is riddled with Scripture!

Have fun; draw a picture of whatever God
gives to you. Or doodle, it's a great way to
open opportunities for anything to happen.
Just remember, color inside the lines.

13

READ,
READ,
READ

I promise this WILL NOT be a long chapter. (Because I don't like to read...)

So do it. Discipline yourself to start your day with scripture, or a devotional attached to scripture. There are a ton of great devotions out there. If you're a technology person, there are even cheap (and some free) apps available. My personal feeling on reading is that there is nothing like paper in your hand that you can rip, tear, cry on, wipe greasy, bacon-laden fingers or donut sprinkles on, or, in all seriousness, journal on in the margins whatever God has showed you. We do however live in an electronic world now (which thankfully screen protectors really do help disperse bacon grease). As for Bibles, devotionals and other scriptural documents, my take is that there is only one thing holy and that's God. Don't turn your Bible into God. Mark it up, use it; throw it if you get angry at a passage that hurts today, bless it, anoint it, write in it. It's your bridge between God and your world. Use it in whatever way makes you feel alive with God. Some may disagree. But as I stated earlier, anything you place in your life more important than drawing closer to God, becomes God. I promise you the publishing companies don't keep their printing presses in Holy temples only to be worked on by priests.

Do whatever works for you when it comes to digesting and reflecting on God's word every day.

Now down to the serious stuff. That was all the 'have to' stuff. Getting your day started off with God is extremely important when you are trying to center your day on the cross with all the distractions that are around us. Satan thinks he's in control, but news for him; we are training up another one to stand against him, right now. Yes, you! Grab your iPhone, unlock it, turn the camera on (selfie mode) and look at that gorgeous image God created to serve Him. Now say, "I am a warrior for Christ."

Other great resources are available, such as Bible app programs for your computer, some are free and again, some require an investment, but open up opportunities for online book downloads to build an electronic library of so many resources such as commentaries, illustrative dictionaries, sermon helps and so on. Many of these programs are specifically designed for pastoral preparation, so they include great search tools to cross reference scriptures and historical periods of time, word studies and more. Get familiar. I use one known as Wordsearch, which over the years I have built into a quite an extensive data base tool. They even have a whole humor section for us light-hearted preachers that prefer live audiences over catatonic clusters of parishioners. In other words, keep them awake!

Okay, so it's important to read, but what else? It's equally important to stay current: stay up on current political, social and community happenings, because that is what you are ministering to; not Jeremiah building a wall, or Samson cutting his hair. You are dealing with the world just as Jesus did, so be relatable. If you have no clue what is going on in the world, how can you minister to one's fears, worries and anxieties regarding where their next meal is coming from or when interest rates are going to make getting a second job a necessity or about the divorce rate soaring due to military lifestyles. (Or whatever their concerns are; I just made up examples obviously.) The point is, people need their hearts ministered to so they can join your crusade with the knowledge that Christ is capable of taking care of them and then they can help you take care of others. You might even get a day off, if that happens. So, reading, on your day off: read, read, read.

Just be careful in presenting your view on something sensitive, unless you are backed by the word of God through it. Being a conservative or a liberal in some communities may still get you hung out to dry with an empty church to pay for to boot. Jesus simply knew what was going on with His surroundings: the Jews, the Romans, Sanhedrin and so on; enough to understand what problems His people may be experiencing. Then He could minister to them without harm.

(I said short, but this may actually be the longest chapter.)

The best advice when it comes to reading is having credible sources, don't read for quantity read for quality and purpose, whether it be five verses or one psalm, one short story or an interesting journal article. Reading should not be a chore, but a tool to draw closer to the cross and God; yes, centering on the cross and its purpose, always. Don't be afraid to read the Quran, or other books of opposition. (*Gulp!*) You as well need to know your opponents, right? Satan has read God's word, that's the only way he has the ability to distort its truth, after all!

Happy reading! Send me some good stuff you run across.

14

PULLING OUT ALL THE TOOLS

ONE OF MY FAVORITE MOVIE SCENES COMES FROM "*INDIANA JONES, Raiders of the Lost Ark,*" is the one in which Dr. Jones has just eluded the Russians while they are trying to capture an artifact from a warehouse in the desert. Dr. Jones finds himself in a Nuclear test site which is about to detonate, when he looks off to his side in a mock kitchen setting to find an old *Frigidaire* in the corner. Knowing it is lined with superior material like lead; he tears open the door, removes all the inner components and climbs inside within seconds of a nuclear blast. Moments later we observe Dr. Jones ferociously being whisked across the desert with tumble weeds and the remnants of a nuked town, ending with Dr. Jones opening the refrigerator door and crawling out to safety.

What does that have to do with ministry you might ask? A good minister, in order to save a soul, uses whatever he is able to further the Gospel effectively, this includes ingenuity and, well, in Dr. Jones' case, an ice box did the trick.

The title, "Pulling out all the tools," means we shall persevere in all that we attempt to accomplish. We want the very best for God's people and we will do whatever is necessary to see that to fruition. (We certainly don't want to be on the corner handing out SPF 10,000 to the ones we couldn't save.) After all, Jesus said so in Matthew 28, remember. Go into all nations preaching the Gospel (paraphrased) because you and I have both memorized that most important piece of scripture before we even left that chapter, we need to gather our tools to go. (Please don't grab the Frigidaire!)

"Jesus said go"

He also said, "All authority has been given to me
in heaven and on earth." Matthew 28:18 NKJV

Again, this is the opening monologue to the Great Commission. Authority is a powerful word when it's from God. It isn't like your old boss saying I have the authority to send you home because of your attitude today. No, it means complete control in its entirety of a situation that you might want to listen up about. God, if you are fully submitted to Him, has that authority over you and should be considered authoritative. Jesus says to "Go" and we should do just that, equipping ourselves with all that we can to be successful for Him.

So, my question to you in this hour is, are you considering arm chair ministry? Like a nice leather office chair style, or is a lazy boy perhaps more your style? When Jesus said *Go,* did something ignite inside of you, pushing you to leave the comfortable imprint of your office chair and *Go*? That is what we are talking about. Along with that again, taking all the tools with us we might need to be successful in going, because Jesus said *Go*. God told Jesus to *Go* and where did He end up? At the finish line, the cross, where He declared with all authority from heaven and earth that "It" was finished. The plan for salvation was finished by His last breath. So, are we to be concerned with our part? (Yes, we are!) Our part, if you haven't figured it out, is what Matthew 28 asks of us, to go into all nations teaching about Jesus and what He was able to do for us to secure eternity. His tools were with Him and so shall ours (His) be.

We are out to make disciples. The cool part is you don't need to stop at the local hardware store for a tool box for our tools. Our tools are very simple: the word of God by our side and in our hearts, (being equipped to make disciples), and the modeled and closely studied actions of Jesus Christ who showed us how to *Go*.

What was His method? Please, at this point, go back and read the Gospels Matthew, Mark, Luke and John if they are still foggy. Study His actions with intensity.

1. He met people where they were
2. He genuinely loved people.
3. He broke bread with people.
4. He cried and laughed with people.
5. He was relatable with people.
6. He healed people.
7. He cared for people's needs.
8. He served people.
9. He listened to people.
10. He prayed over people.
11. He was selfless before people.
12. He united with people.
13. He judged no people.
14. He asked for forgiveness for people.
15. He died for all people.

Not an all-inclusive list of what He did, but as you read through the gospels reflect on these attributes. He would not start this process without showing us how to do it. So, we should stop trying to reinvent the process and follow what Jesus did.

We have all seen the bumper stickers and decals WWJD with the embossed fish around it symbolizing "What Would Jesus Do?" The better question for a Pastor is WDJD- "What *Did* Jesus Do?" What you see above is what He did; just exactly what He did. You read through the Gospel accounts; that's what He did. He genuinely loved people enough to obediently die for them despite how they felt about Him.

Could you or I have that same capacity of love within us? (Might require quite a large tool box to carry that one!)

15

GOD, THE SUPREME

HAVE YOU EVER BEEN TO THE EMERGENCY ROOM FOR AN INJURY AND one of the first things the team asks you is on a scale of 1-10, what is your level of pain? I hope you have never had that unpleasantry, but if you have, you would know they use that as a tool to assess how soon you should be seen. If we consider how much physical pain Jesus endured during the crucifixion, do you think His pain would have been a priority to the physicians that day? How about to the Father? I would think so. After all, He was skinned alive, spit upon, dragged through the dirt, forced to carry that heavy cross up Calgary to His destination there. Now, here is the problem: that speaks only of the physical pain that He endured. The emotional and spiritual pain I call immeasurable. Close your eyes for a minute (well, after you read this paragraph that is) and envision Niagara Falls for a moment. Standing in the ravine at the bottom and there is no water flowing, it suddenly has become a barren, parched wasteland. Yet, at the top of the cliff, you can hear the tremendous rumbling energy stirring up and building, as if you are walking through the parted Red Sea during the exodus, perhaps. As the minutes linger on and turn into a few hours, you see the water begin to crest as if no more can be held back. You know what lies ahead, you know what is being asked of you; you're tired, beaten and unrecognizable in your body anymore. You were sent to save the world from its curse of sin and that sin (in the form of rushing water) is about to come plowing down upon you with such a tremendous and unbearable force. It becomes too much for any human to possibly bear (yet HE did it for you). As the last few moments roll by, it becomes as if the water building above is instantly released with all its potential force. The water comes plummeting down and crashes upon you and you have no choice but to take its full course of impact onto your body. At the very moment this occurs your last bit of energy is expelled exclaiming, "It is finished!" You have just barely experienced a glimpse into the reality of what the sin of the world: past, present and future, looks like bearing down upon one responsible, obedient loving person. But it's not someone else's sin only we are talking about, it's yours and mine, it's your family, it's the unsaved, the lost, the seemingly underserving, it is the drug addicts, the gamblers, the child molesters, the pornographers, it is the unimaginable. It is all sin, accepted in full by the savior, so that you would have a choice to either follow Him (love Him) or deny Him. Yes, you still have a choice to love Jesus or not. The payment has no payback terms. The check was written, cleared the bank with no hold, and your debts completely paid, absolutely no strings or conditions other than to love Him fully.

So has the emergency room position changed, did Jesus move up on the pain scale any? Are we still considering physical pain over what pain Jesus truly endured and His Father orchestrated for you and me? He died of heart failure perhaps, not the physical wounds, of course that's not scriptural, but certainly perceivable.

This now becomes the small piece of possible honor and glory we could give back to the Father for what Jesus has done freely for us. We simply can serve Him and tell others about Him so those that don't know Him, or have been led astray by wolves in sheep's clothing, can claim their inheritance as well. That's it. He wants everyone to know about Him and the gift He has left behind, called salvation; an eternal inheritance as a child of God and future resident in His heavenly kingdom.

The spiritual pain scale to me now seems quite the priority; to love Him and pay tribute to Him in even the minutest of ways, to be a ministry leader to whatever degree, whether it is serving in a food line on Friday nights sharing the gift of love to those less fortunate, being involved in global ministry or street evangelism. For me, it was just becoming a Pastor, being open, fully exposed to be used by the Holy Spirit as needed, and to be as obedient as possible simply to honor Him for what He has done for me. The God I chose to serve and the God I chose to inspire you about. If the crucifixion and death of Jesus did not inspire you enough, then perhaps the more realistic image I attempted to portray for you would spark a deeper desire within you. To serve Him, love Him and be obedient to His commands.

It takes a lot, but does it really, in comparison with what He has given us first and foremost, before we were even born? He is the one who gave unconditionally. This is just an *Aha!* chapter to reflect upon; motivation to move. He told us to *Go* and so many of us are not. That is called complacency and, well, not very God-honoring, if you ask me. One person, one view, one interpretation, but still the only one I will ever serve. That tug should hopefully be in full force by now, but you and I still have a lot of work to get done so that when we do get going nobody is shorted their opportunity at salvation.

16

PREPARING FOR
THE BATTLEFIELD

VEN BEFORE SOMEONE BECOMES A PASTOR, WE HAVE THE POTENTIAL TO minister. We can love people. Hear a theme throughout this book yet? Love people: the great commandment of loving the Lord and loving your neighbor as yourself. It is what we are called to do regardless if we are just new Christians or fully blown denominational leaders of a church. Love people. Matthew 25:34-46 gives an outline of how to love someone.

"Then the King will say to those on His right hand, 'Come, you blessed of My Father, inherit the kingdom prepared for you from the foundation of the world: for I was hungry and you gave Me food; I was thirsty and you gave Me drink; I was a stranger and you took Me in; I was naked and you clothed Me; I was sick and you visited Me; I was in prison and you came to Me.' "Then the righteous will answer Him, saying, 'Lord, when did we see You hungry and feed You, or thirsty and give You drink? When did we see You a stranger and take You in, or naked and clothe You? Or when did we see You sick, or in prison, and come to You?' And the King will answer and say to them, 'Assuredly, I say to you, inasmuch as you did it to one of the least of these My brethren, you did it to Me.' "Then He will also say to those on the left hand, 'Depart from Me, you cursed, into the everlasting fire prepared for the devil and his angels: for I was hungry and you gave Me no food; I was thirsty and you gave Me no drink; I was a stranger and you did not take Me in, naked and you did not clothe Me, sick and in prison and you did not visit Me.' "Then they also will answer Him, saying, 'Lord, when did we see You hungry or thirsty or a stranger or naked or sick or in prison, and did not minister to You?' Then He will answer them, saying, 'Assuredly, I say to you, inasmuch as you did not do it to one of the least of these, you did not do it to Me.' And these will go away into everlasting punishment, but the righteous into eternal life.'" Matthew 25:34-46 NKJV

If you ever come into dispute with someone, this is always a good question to ask, "Who defined love?" Most will say Webster's dictionary, or the younger generation may say *Google!* In actuality, God's standard is the measurement of love, just as evil is outlined throughout the Bible. So, the battlefield may seem less intimidating knowing that all you must do to start ministry is go and love people. Food, clothing, a drink, a conversation; as we take another view at the Jesus model (the Gospel), meeting people where they are comes first, followed by getting them to where Jesus wants them. If someone is suffering from addiction they don't need a cheeseburger, although they may, as a step to get to the next point. They need to know someone is listening to them and that they are being heard (loved) first. That's it. Be a servant today, work towards discerning someone's needs. Don't guess at their needs but be intentional about trying to understand where someone is in life and where they want to get to, and praise the Lord in all circumstances good and bad. Good that you were placed there, bad that things can get better for someone now. It takes a conscious effort to get to know someone. It takes empathy to connect, relate and apply a loving touch to someone's life which shows somebody that you truly can be beside them, walking with them or at least partially feeling their pain or joys.

Pray, pray, pray that God will lead you towards someone that can use you today, right now. Book mark this chapter and *Go* as He commands; take a couple dollars with you to super-size someone's value fries today. Hold someone's hand (with permission) or give them a hug. Get to know someone today like you have never known someone before. That closet, where everything is secretly kept, stirring and waiting to be released on someone who can minister like Jesus did.

Did I mention prayer? Yes, definitely do nothing without asking the Father first for His blessing and anointing to fall upon your environment. Why would He deny you that? He won't, I promise you. Confess your own shortcomings today; ask the Lord to guard you from the enemy and have the wisdom and ability to use whatever situation to His Glory.

Remember what a battlefield looks like from old movies (or if you had the opportunity to serve during wartime), sometimes there are defined lines and sometimes there are not. Sometimes your enemy is right beside you waiting to strike and sometimes they are far from sight. The enemy we face is not of the flesh, we should remember. Nobody that I know of wakes up to say I want to be a rapist today, or a pedophile, or become addicted to opioids. It becomes a dark place filled with a false necessity to continue on in life - that is a lost soul's reality. The thing to remember is the old saying, "There are no atheists in foxholes." That means everyone, when pushed to the extreme of their environment, has something they feel they can turn to for an answer: a deity, a memory, a glimmer of something that brings a piece of value to their lives. It could be something as trivial as a four-leaf clover, or a lucky horseshoe. It becomes our job to help discover what brings comfort to someone in that time of need such as the "foxhole". Without compromising our own beliefs, we turn back to our ability to stand beside someone in that dark hour.

The battlefield we fight on starts in the spiritual realm; so should yours. Yes, there's that word prayer again; praying for God's discernment, His guidance and direction.

> His direction and guidance,
> His protection.
> They can accomplish so much.

These are great places to start as you gear up to go into battle. The spiritual realm is just that, a spirit that will attach to an individual guiding their actions to ungodly territory. The good news is that if there is a battle going on, there is a great chance at victory. It is when the silence sets in that things become seemingly more difficult, but even then, anything is possible. We have to be aware of when the battle in the mind between right and wrong, good and evil, slows or stops.

Let them talk; let them tell you where they are in the moment of need. The battle, after all, is theirs, not yours; you're just trying to help them claim victory. If you're able to pray with them then pray; prayer brings confidence and security to many. Prayer opens opportunity for a voice to be heard from the battlefield. Start the prayer and encourage participation and eventually encourage closing the prayer by your new partner. This is just one perspective on battlefield strategies, one that has worked for me and one I encourage you to practice among others that exist. Don't limit your options. The dark prince of this world is dangerous and always trying new things. Stay on top of your game!

FOLLOWING PASSIONATE
LEADERS

WE ARE NOT REFERRING TO INSTAGRAM HERE; FACEBOOK TWEETS, likes, followers or whatnots have no bearing here. (Ok, I'm not *that* old, I know its Facebook #hashtags really. Stay off my Insta's would you?!) Social media has no place in God's kingdom unless you are sharing the Love of God there.

This is a means of discovery. It is a means to find out a style or styles that you feel comfortable surrounding yourself with. It can also become a trial and error situation. It becomes about Godly people and how they impact your life; about the way you share the Gospel and the methodology you choose to take when loving people. Good leaders, good evangelists, good men and women of God passionately doing the Lord's work can be enough to sometimes to spark more passion inside oneself. We can never have enough passion to share God's love with people, can we?

The world is filled with celebrities that influence so many facets of life, even politics, (go figure), but are the majority qualified to have a political voice because they starred in an Emmy award winning sitcom? We have celebrities that provide negative influences but seem to have lucky charms and can do no wrong regardless of their behavior. We also have celebrities, sports figures, political figures, and so on that present very good intentions and represent high moral and ethical standards. Just as there are negative influences, there are positive figures in the world as well. We can learn a lot from both. The world of ministry, although less alarming, still has the same concerns as the secular world.

As I was building on this chapter in my head, I was considering all the different arguments that could arise such as copying someone's technique, mimicking, or whatever you want to call it; taking shortcuts. My theology is that nothing in ministry is new; it has all been tried and tested in the past. True godly people don't have a single issue sharing their thoughts or actions if it continues to further the Gospel successfully. Motivation comes from seeing success and when you observe one's style of presentation and feel comfortable in its surroundings, then why should that not influence your style and purpose?

Now there is a lot more to following a person of influence than just looking at their style, their effectiveness goes a long way. If I were to present material in a way that allows more people to grasp the content, then I would say I am successful. If I present material and even bore myself after ten minutes, there may be something to improve upon regarding the presentation. Passionate people present powerful and passionate messages that change lives.

Following someone with passion also requires you to look at their motives. An individual can be motivated by personal success, financial gain and even simply the act of performing (we call that attractivism). This technique requires a very delicate balance of presentation in order to avoid becoming solely an entertainer rather than an effective presenter or minister of the Gospel. The Gospel message is always the most important part of our ministry, never to be compromised.

"As we have said before, so now I say again, if
anyone preaches any other gospel to you than
what you have received, let him be accursed."
Galatians 1:9 NKJV

As this passage of scripture states, you probably don't want to mess up what the Gospel speaks of because of a flashy phrase or catchy talk point.

Leaders are leaders because:

1. At some point a group of individuals have recognized their impact on a purpose.
2. They have proven to be successful in their endeavors by means of accomplishment.
3. They are perhaps powerful and/or very knowledgeable people in a given number of areas of expertise, such as exegetical studies, theology or apologetics, missionaries, or more.

Tried and tested in short, I trust their direction, motivates and intentions; they are leaders, in my perspective. I have certain leaders that I look up to as well-respected, in my opinion, and, in a few cases, the world's opinion. Please, do your due diligence; make sure the leaders you choose to follow don't just hold an entertainment value. Look for the meat and potatoes, the backbone that proves them worthy of your time and study. God is good at providing shepherds even to His shepherds, but Satan is also good at herding the wolves in sheep's clothing.

Before you start studying an individual for their impact on your ministry, hear their testimony; how did God work in their life, or did He at all? Where did they study, what contributions did they give to God's ministry? Did they lead a global initiative to present new Bible translations around the world? Did they begin a ministry to feed homeless or clothe poverty-stricken regions? Or did they simply earn a great living becoming a good orator and lean on that for their existence?

There are a lot of questions to dig through, and if you are anything like I was when I first started out, I didn't know which question to ask to get the most out of my efforts. Even still, I have a few leaders that I just enjoy listening to because they speak well. I have since given them credit for the knowledge they do have, but others rank higher in credibility, with lesser of a presentation. Just be careful; dig passionately and find figures that inspire you to continue to push through the trials we come across and the attacks that muffle our efforts. If you are interested in some of the leaders that provide value and sustenance in my life, then I will be certain to supply those to you by email correspondence which again can be found in the beginning and ending of this resource.

18

ETERNAL VALUE: KNOWING YOUR WORTH

I HAVE BEEN LYING HERE IN BED STARING AT THE CEILING FOR SOME TIME now thinking about this chapter. It's called knowing your worth for a reason. There, perhaps, is no more a cherished job than saving lives for eternity. (Keeping them alive in the physical realm may have a little purpose, I suppose.)

Going back to my childhood days, I recall some very memorable times that seemed boring to me as a kid but hold a place of treasure in my heart today. They were times spent with my father just doing whatever. One of the things he enjoyed was listening to old time radio shows. One in particular stood out to me, a comedy that ran in the 1940's with great success called, "Fibber McGee and Molly." They were great at not only telling stories but making them come alive. Of course, most of them were humorous and upbeat and very entertaining, which caught my eye (or ears) the most. Later in my years I could begin to put together the magic of what was transpiring over the radio waves: a team of talented individuals, dedicated to making the show as lively, realistic and entertaining as possible. The real magic lay in their seemingly limitless imagination and skill. Sound effects from thunder, screeching car tires or crowds of people on the streets, all originated from the space of perhaps a medium size studio. A team dedicated to a cause, this cause, entertainment. Long before GIF's, emoji's, MP4 files and iTunes, there were minds that could create sound effects from odd implements. I now lay here envisioning sheet metal, rubber mallets, hollow tubes of various sizes, planks of wood and kitchen utensils that generated enough vibrant and realistic sounds; sounds that could stimulate the imagination into being in a place of realistic storytelling. Wow! A team dedicated with passion and desire to accomplish such a feat, so that I could be entertained for the thirty minutes perched in front of a radio with Dad. Not only the thirty minutes though, as I sit here and recollect in this moment, but a lifetime of memories. That's impact!

Now Preach, you ask, *what in the world are you getting at?* Glad you asked! Each of those individuals knew their role and executed to make something happen. They had value and purpose whether they were aware of it or not.

You as a minister of the Gospel have value and purpose far superior to the confines of a thirty-minute radio spot. Yours has eternal value; you will have a responsibility to put all those sound effects into motion. You have active participants to help you along the way, but please know your value. I don't want you to think you are alone as you move into ministry; keep this mindset. Your value to the lost, to serving God is immeasurable when you do it for His glory alone. The moment you attempt any credit, well, you might has well have struck a hammer on a piece of sheet metal for the noise of a baby crying, instead you got thunder. You might have messed up the whole show in one action; that is how valuable you and your ministry will become. Knowing your value to the Kingdom can not only be a bit overwhelming, it can be priceless when it comes to motivating the soul to *Go* and proclaim the gospel message. How does it motivate you?

If you at this point haven't gone into any study of eternal destiny (as we mentioned earlier it is nothing to play around with) take some time to do so. Study about eternity from scripture and the consequences of denying Jesus; look no further than the Gospels. Motivation comes from knowing where an unsaved individual will spend the rest of their existence. Let me make an effort to paint a very broad image of the surroundings. Eternity outside of heaven is HOT. Real or not, we have seen early cartoon depictions of Satan with His fiery horns pierced upon his head, pitch fork in hand surrounded by a background of fire and flames. In fact, that is probably the easiest part to envision. What lay behind the scenes is torment, pain and suffering repeatedly over and over forever. If that were not enough to motivate you, imagine an environment with absolutely no trace of love- not one ounce of it- no hope, no promise of tomorrow, not even a trace representation of God existing, and God is the origin of Love.

If there isn't enough motivation in that paragraph just go ahead and step away from the book. (Step away slowly, easy, you got this. There's always basket weaving classes.) Okay, serious, allow it to motivate you and to move you. God, you, and your team want everyone to experience the glory of God's kingdom, let's not turn one soul over to the enemy. If it benefits your ministry, turn this book into a small group study. Take your team with you. You will gather a valuable source of lay people, pastoral friends and just wise and knowledgeable street folks who have been turned off by the church. Use all of them to further the Gospel.

Take heed as I share this with you also; the second your worth, your ministry, is placed on a pedestal, you will notice that you're able to be knocked down easier. Stay at street level with your legs planted firmly on the ground. A humble spirit can take your ministry far when you're open to those around you supporting you and working alongside you. My ministry and I want you to succeed. God wants you to succeed. My prayer moving forward is that happens for you. My prayer is that you hear God tell you to go purchase this book (not for my benefit) but because you want to serve Him and you are valuable to Him in so many ways. You are His child and He will bless you. You will experience valleys; hard times that seem impassible. That impassible feeling comes because you are trying to make possible what is only possible through God. God will call into reality what is not reality. He will move mountains and straighten crooked paths. He is capable of all things and He provides those same divine gifts to us all through Him. Know your worth to Him and know your team's worth to Him additionally.

19

PUTTING IT ALL TOGETHER

T HIS CHAPTER COULD BE ONE WORD OR MANY PARAGRAPHS. PUTTING everything we touched on together can boil down to trusting everything into the faithful hands of a loving Father. Equip yourself with as much knowledge as possible. Share your newly gained wisdom with those that influence your ministry. Love your ministry and nurture it, taking care of every detail that surrounds it. Your ministry team is another ministry for you; a ministry you will be nurturing to maturity as you grow together in experience.

Putting it all together should include unified prayer with your team for the purpose of glorifying God and for His will to be done

"For where two or three are gathered
together in My name, I am there in the
midst of them." Matthew 18:20 NKJV

Pray always, ask boldly, always asking for God's will to be done. Honor Him in your prayers and petitions. Glorify and praise Him in your prayers. You are not praying; you are having a relationship with the Creator. Whether you are casually talking to Him while driving down the road, or you are in a prayer closet battle, bringing major issues before His throne, share what is on your heart. As stated earlier, He already knows anyway. You can't run, you can't hide.

Consult your resources frequently. Utilize all the weapons in your arsenal for godly results. Always think in terms of what Jesus did and what He would have done in any given situation, and when in doubt, consult the truth. If the Bible confirms it, then you're not going to fail in your efforts.

We have talked about a lot of things together. Some may seem discouraging and impossible, others may empower you to get started or change directions in your ministry right now. That knowledge encourages me greatly; know that prayer is the foundation behind all of it. God has given each of us an opportunity to serve Him and He desperately wants you to.

One thing we perhaps did not elaborate on is the ending of Matthew 28 which has a lot of significance in my personal ministry. Jesus says, "And lo I will be with you always until the end of the age." Here you go. Jesus the Lord of all creation, the Son of Man is with us through everything. Do you truly think He would allow you to fail? Not a chance. There may be lessons along the way on the paths we choose incorrectly but He will be with us through every situation.

APPENDIXES
(Important snippets to keep close)

BIBLE TRANSLATIONS:

Word for Word Translations: The word-for-word versions most accurately follow the Hebrew, Aramaic and Greek texts.

King James Version KJV

The KJV is the first version of Scripture authorized by the Protestant church and commissioned by England's King James I.

New King James Version NKJV

The NKJ is a modern language update of the original King James Version. It retains much of the traditional interpretation and sentence structure of the KJV.

A More Modern Equivalent Word for Word:

American Standard Version ASV

The American Standard Version is a revised version of the King James Version completed in 1885. (Wikipedia) The ASV was the basis of four revisions. They were the RSV, 1971, the Amp Bible, 1965, the NASB, 1995, and the Recovery Version, 1999.

New Revised Standard NRS

The New Revised Standard is a popular translation that follows in the traditions of the King James and RSV. With the goal of preserving the best of the older versions with modern English applied.

Revised Standard Version RSV

The RSV is a revision of the King James Version, the Revised Version, and American Standard Version. This text is intended for both private reading and public worship.

New American Standard Bible NAS

The NAS is written in a formal style but is more readable than the KJV. It is highly respected as the most literal English translation of the Bible.

New International Version NIV

The NIV offers a balance between a word-for-word and thought-for-thought translation and is considered by many as a highly accurate and smooth-reading version of the Bible in modern English.

Meaning for Meaning Translations: Provide more up to date language. Not the best for providing sound doctrine as opposed to Word for Word translations; more valuable for making scripture understandable.

Good News Translation GNT

The Good News Translation was first published in 1976 by the American Bible Society in a "common language." The simple, everyday language makes it especially popular for children and those learning English.

GOD'S WORD Translation GW

GOD'S WORD Translation (GW) Readable and reliable, accurately translates the meaning of the original texts into clear, everyday language.

New Living Translation NLT

Using modern English, the NLT focused on producing clarity in the meaning of the text rather than creating a literal, word-for-word equivalence. Their goal creates a clear, readable translation while remaining faithful to original texts.

Paraphrased Translations: These are easier versions to read- their goal is modern language interpretation with a warning that a bit of poetic license gives way to proper interpretation. Use these translations in conjunction with a more meaning by meaning or word for word aide.

The Message Bible MSG

The Message is a paraphrase from the original languages written by Eugene, H. Peterson. The Message provides a fresh and unique Bible-reading experience.

The Living Bible

A Paraphrased translation with the intent of saying what the writers of scripture meant and said in as simplistic means as possible.

Literal Translation Seeking Precision Wording: It seeks to be transparent to the original text, letting the reader see as directly as possible the structure and meaning of the original.

English Standard Version ESV

The ESV Bible is a relatively new Bible translation that combines word-for-word precision and accuracy with literary excellence, beauty, and readability.

Faithful and Original Translation

The Holman Christian Standard Bible (HCSB) is a trusted, original translation of God's Word. Each word must reflect clear, contemporary English and each word must be faithful to the original languages of the Bible.

Holman Christian Standard Bible CSB

The HCS is a highly readable, accurate translation written in modern English. It is published by Holman Bible Publishers, the oldest Bible publisher in America.

BOOKS OF INTEREST

Arthur, K. *How to Study Your Bible*. Harvest House Publishers, 2001.

Barna, G. *The Power of Vision: Discover and Apply God's Plan for Your Life and Ministry*. ReadHowYouWant.com, Limited, 2010.

Bickel, B. and S. Jantz. *Listening to God: Experience His Presence Every Day*. Barbour Publishing, Incorporated, 2012.

Blanchard, K. and R. McNeal. "Practicing Greatness: 7 Disciplines of Extraordinary Spiritual Leaders." *Zeitschrift Für Celtische Philologie* 58 (2006): 225-27. http://eu.wiley.com/remtitle. cgi?ISBN=0470893915.

Boa, Kenneth. D. *Conformed to His Image*. Zondervan, 2009.

Bonhoeffer, D. *Discipleship*. Fortress Press, 2003.

Bruce, F.F. *Paul: Apostle of the Heart Set Free*. Eerdmans Publishing Company, 2000.

Burpo, T. *Heaven Is for Real: A Little Boy's Astounding Story of His Trip to Heaven and Back: Conversation Guide*. Thomas Nelson, 2011.

Carothers, M. *Prison to Praise*. BookBaby, 1970.

Chambers, Oswald. "My Utmost for His Highest." *Grand Rapids Michigan Oswald Chambers Publications Association* (1992).

Chan, F. and M. Beuving. *Multiply: Disciples Making Disciples*. David C. Cook, 2012.

Dockery, D.S. *Christian Leadership Essentials: A Handbook for Managing Christian Organizations.* B&H Adademic, 2011.

Donald, M. "Prayer Life of Jesus [Paperback]." (http://www.christianbookstore. net/prayer-life-of-jesus-by-macintyre-donald/catalog-39706/.

Duvall, J.S. and J.D. Hays. *Grasping God's Word: A Hands-on Approach to Reading, Interpreting, and Applying the Bible.* Zondervan, 2005.

Duvall, J.S. and J.D. Hays. *Journey into God's Word: Your Guide to Understanding and Applying the Bible.* Zondervan, 2008.

Earley, D. and R. Dempsey. *Disciple Making Is . . .: How to Live the Great Commission with Passion and Confidence.* B&H Publishing Group, 2013.

Earley, D. and B. Gutierrez. *Ministry Is...: How to Serve Jesus with Passion and Confidence.* B&H Publishing Group, 2010.

Earley, D. and D. Wheeler. *Evangelism Is—: How to Share Jesus with Passion and Confidence.* B&H Publishing Group, 2010.

Frazee, R. and R. Larson. *Believe Study Guide: Living the Story of the Bible to Become Like Jesus.* Zondervan, 2015.

Graham, B. *The Reason for My Hope: Salvation.* Thomas Nelson, 2013.

Graham, F. and D.L. Toney. *Through My Father's Eyes.* Thomas Nelson, 2018.

Hull, B. *The Complete Book of Discipleship: On Being and Making Followers of Christ.* NavPress Publishing Group, 2014.

Lewis, C.S. *Mere Christianity.* HarperCollins, 2001.

Macarthur, J. "Pastoral Ministry: How to Shepherd Biblically [Hardcover]." (http://www.christianbookstore.net/pastoral-ministry-how-to-shepherd-biblically-by/catalog-24525/.

Malphurs, A. *Being Leaders: The Nature of Authentic Christian Leadership.* Baker Publishing Group, 2003.

Malphurs, A. *Advanced Strategic Planning: A 21st-Century Model for Church and Ministry Leaders.* Baker Publishing Group, 2013.

McDill, W. *The 12 Essential Skills for Great Preaching - Second Edition.* B&H Publishing Group, 2006.

McNeal, R. and K. Blanchard. *Practicing Greatness: 7 Disciplines of Extraordinary Spiritual Leaders.* Wiley, 2010.

Miller, S. *D.L. Moody on Spiritual Leadership.* Moody Publishers, 2008.

Murray, A. *Humility.* ReadHowYouWant.com, Limited, 2009.

Myra, H.L. and M. Shelley. *The Leadership Secrets of Billy Graham.* Zondervan, 2005.

Nichols, Stephen. "Bonhoeffer on the Christian Life: From the Cross, for the World." *Wheaton Illinois Crossway* (2013).

Spurgeon, C. *An All-around Ministry: Addresses to Ministers and Students.* CreateSpace Independent Publishing Platform, 2014.

Spurgeon, Charles. "Lectures to My Students: Complete and Unabridged." (http://www.langtoninfo.com/showitem.aspx?isbn=0310329116.

Teykl, T. and L. Ponder. *The Presence Based Church.* Prayer Point Press, 2003.

Toler, Stan. "Practical Guide to Pastoral Ministry." (http://self-publish-ebooks.com/books/view/553013.

Towns, E.L., M. Couch, and E.E. Hindson. *The Gospel of John: Believe and Live*. AMG Publishers, 2002.

Tozer, A.W. *The Pursuit of God*. 2017.

Tozer, A.W. and J.L. Snyder. *The Crucified Life: How to Live out a Deeper Christian Experience*. Gospel Light, 2011.

Warren, R. *The Purpose-Driven Life: What on Earth Am I Here For?*: Zondervan, 2003.

Warren, R. *The Purpose Driven Church: Growth without Compromising Your Message and Mission*. Zondervan, 2007.

Whitney, D.S. *Spiritual Disciplines for the Christian Life*. NavPress, 2014.

Yount, W.R. *The Teaching Ministry of the Church*. B&H Academic, 2008.

CLERGY WORTH STUDYING

Good, bad or indifferent these ministers and leaders are worth studying for their contributions or lack of contributions. I am not here to persuade anyone's ministry but just ask that you do your due diligence in discovering for yourself what you find significant. Listed in no specific order:

Reverend* Pastor *Doctor* Bishop* Etc.
(Excluded for simplicity)

Billy Graham	Rod Parsley
Pat Robertson	Robert Tilton
Martin Luther King Jr.	Brian Houston
Joel Osteen	John Maxwell
John Piper	Martin Luther
Rick Warren	Francis Chan
Jerry Fawell	Erwin Lutzer
Dietrich Bonhoeffer	John Newton
Dwight L. Moody	R.C. Sproul
Charles Swindoll	David Platt
John Hagee	Louie Giglio
Karl Barth	Derek Prince
Jonathan Edwards	Martin Niemoller
Charles Spurgeon	Nicole Lamarche
Charles Stanley	T.D. Jakes
Adrian Rogers	Ravi Zacharias
David Wilkerson	Joseph Prince
David Jeremiah	Tony Evans
Andrew Murray	Joyce Meyers
Earl Paulk	Ray Hammond
Rob Bell	Myself (Of course)

DEVOTIONALS

In the interest of current material being accessed, I recommend using a web search option to find specific devotionals that are current and effective for your needs. I have my favorites such as Billy Graham and David Jeremiah but please utilize the most recent that serve your needs at the time. There are also web services and phone apps that can provide convenient devotional material daily.

HOLY SPIRIT

We can be certain that if we are followers of Christ we should be practicing these fruits on a continuous basis. They should become the baseline of your ministry.

Fruit of the Holy Spirit

Love
Joy
Peace
Longsuffering
Kindness
Goodness
Faithfulness
Gentleness
Self-control

Gifts are not always evident to followers. God has His methods (to which I am not God so I will not question) and oftentimes gifts are received by some to whom it may, for the purpose of God's will, be necessary and to others not. Do not be discouraged if you do not experience a specific gift during a given period of your ministry. Know that God's gift of a plan for you is more than enough to see you through any and all situations.

Gifts of the Holy Spirit

The Word of Knowledge
The Word of Wisdom
The Gift of Prophecy
The Gift of Faith

Eric Catron

The Gifts of Healings
The Working of Miracles
The Discerning of Spirits
Different Kinds of Tongues
The Interpretation of Tongues

PRAYER:

The Lord's Prayer was worthy of putting in a quick reference since we can see the significance of Jesus words written in red. He taught His disciples to pray and we should take caution to use His teachings in addition to our own daily conversations with the Father.

The Lord's Prayer is a pattern of prayer found in Matthew 6:9-14 consisting of:

1) Praise His name and who He is.

2) Ask for His righteousness to come upon our world and life. Submit to His WILL

3) Your daily needs provided and Jesus to be with you always.

4) Forgive us of all our wrong ways and help us forgive others.

1) Our Father in heaven, hallowed be your name.

2) Your Kingdom come, your will be done, on earth as in heaven

3) Give us today our daily bread.

4) Forgive us our sins, as we forgive those who sin against us.

5) Keep us safe from Satan and all his world temptations that are not Godly.

6) Proclaim His Glory and His place in your life, giving everything to the rightful owner, God the Father.

5) Lead us not into
temptation,
but deliver us from evil.

6) For the kingdom, the power
and the glory are yours.
Now and forever. Amen.

The significance is being open, in a place of confession, honest and boldly asking for what your heart desires, being certain that your heart aligns with His will as best as possible.

If you still feel drawn to pray, just talk to Him about your worries and your joys. Have a conversation as if you and I were sitting at the coffee table (except you may want to honor Him a bit more than me in this case). You can also just be alone and quiet with Him, which often times brings me the most joy in my time with Him. Just be real, after all, He knows you already!

ROMANS ROAD TO SALVATION

This is a must have in your arsenal of weapons against the enemy. Please don't take these scriptures lightly- know and understand the significance of them. Just throwing them at an unsaved soul moves them no closer to God's kingdom without the whys and truths behind them; it merely gives them a false sense of security. Mark your Bibles from the opposite side and guide your friend through them as they turn the pages to the corresponding scriptures to reflect upon.

I'm considered a good person?

ROMANS 3:23 NKJV – For all have sinned and fall short of the glory of God.
ROMANS 3:10 **NKJV** – As it is written: "there is none righteous, no, not one;
ROMANS 5:12 NKJV – Therefore, just as through one man sin entered the world, and death through sin, and thus death spread to all men, because all sinned–

What about that Sin?

ROMANS 6:23 NKJV – For the wages of sin [is] death, but the gift of God [is] eternal life in Christ Jesus our Lord.

There is hope for me?

ROMANS 5:8 NKJV – But God demonstrates his own love toward us, in that while we were still sinners, Christ died for us.

How do I get Saved?

ROMANS 10:9-10 NKJV – That if you confess with your mouth the lord Jesus and believe in your heart that God has raised him from the dead, you will be saved. for with the heart one believes unto righteousness, and with the mouth confession is made unto salvation

Are we good?

ROMANS 10:13 NKJV – For "whoever calls on the name of the lord shall be saved."

What now?

ROMANS 10:17 NKJV – So then faith [comes] by hearing, and hearing by the word of god.

TYPES OF RELIGIONS

The most common and widely practiced religions in the world are **Christianity, Islam, Nonreligious, Atheism or Agnostic, Hinduism, Chinese, Buddhism.** I will make an attempt to briefly touch on these plus a few additional religions below.

Christianity

(2.1 billion): It's all about one life, the life of Jesus the Son of God. The Bible teaches that because we are sinners by nature and by choice, we have a broken relationship with our Creator. We live out our days seeking fulfillment and meaning in the things that surround us, but the deepest need of the human soul is to be restored to the One who made us. Jesus came to accomplish that restoration.

Islam

(1.3 billion) Allah first created the world and commissioned Adam to tend it. The faith continued through Abraham, followed the line of his son Ishmael and continued through the teachings of Christ until Allah sent his last prophet, Muhammad, to give his final revelation. At age forty, he said he began receiving, via the angel Gabriel, God's revelations. These revelations would be collected into the Qur'an and set a course for what has now become the second most practiced religion of all time. They believe Allah is the holy creator and sustainer of all things. Muslims attribute to Allah most of the qualities Christians bestow on God. Muslims and Christians agree that God is the one and only God, but the God of the Bible is vastly different than the Allah of Islam. For instance, Muslims deny the biblical teaching that God is one being in three persons: Father, Son, and Holy Spirit. (Resource: https://www.imb.org/).

Nonreligious

(Secular/Agnostic/Atheist) (1.1 billion) Atheism is the rejection of any deity or god's existence. Atheism can be stated as the opposite of theism where at least one god exists.

Hinduism

(900 million) An extremely tolerant religion stating (by the famous nonviolent Hindu Mahatma Ghandi) there is only one God but many paths to him. This belief opens up an extremely free choice of belief systems and way of life. In practicality, Hinduism has been a polytheistic system worshiping many gods. A general belief is that a trinity exists- known as Brahma the creator of the universe, Vishnu the preserver of the universe and Shiva the destroyer of the universe.

Chinese traditional religion

(394 million) The Chinese culture has been primarily overseen by a communistic atheist institution prohibiting practicing religion; historically China has been cradled by traditions such as Confucianism and Taoism later to be joined by Buddhism.

Buddhism

376 million Perhaps Buddhism is the most difficult religion to make a universal statement regarding. Buddhist beliefs vary. There are however fundamental concepts associated with its following: to escape suffering and be released from the cycle of rebirth and to reach a level of enlightenment, eternal peace and happiness. The process of being reborn is a fruit of the karma. The four noble truths exist: suffering, desire to cause suffering, freedom from suffering and the eightfold path to gain freedom from suffering.

Primal-indigenous

(300 million) a major belief system in Africa / Asia, these have become outcomes of religious tradition and native world views. Such influences include paganism, shamanism and animism. Primarily henotheistic

(worshiping one god while acknowledging others exist). Living itself is a spiritual act and all existence is thought to be connected including life, death, humans and animals and the spiritual and physical world.

African traditional and Diasporic

(100 million) African Traditional Religions are those practiced by the original inhabitants of Africa and can be divided into four different groups: the Nilo-Saharan, the Niger-Congo, the Khoisan and the Afro-Asiatic Religious Traditions. African Diasporic Religions, on the other hand, are those that developed when the African Traditional Religions practiced by African slaves. There are many different Traditional and Diasporic Religions and each have their own history and specific origin. For the Traditional Religions, one Nilo-Saharan group was monotheistic while another was non theistic (as were the Khoisan groups), the Niger-Congo group was concerned with the manifestation of spirit in nature and the Afro-Asiatic group was henotheistic. (Information retrieved from themonastery.org)

Sikhism

(23 million) A way of life and philosophy well ahead of its time when it was founded over 500 years ago, the Sikh religion today has a following of over twenty million people worldwide. Sikhism preaches a message of devotion and remembrance of God at all times, truthful living, equality of mankind, social justice and denounces superstitions and blind rituals. Sikhism is open to all through the teachings of its 10 Gurus enshrined in the Sikh Holy Book and Living Guru, Sri Guru Granth Sahib. The word 'Sikh' in the Punjabi language means 'disciple', Sikhs are the disciples of God who follow the writings and teachings of the Ten Sikh Gurus. The wisdom of these teachings in Sri Guru Granth Sahib are practical and universal in their appeal to all mankind.

Judaism

(14 million) The Jewish people believe that God is the single creator and animator of the world. He has no helpers, no children and no

enemies. God is the invisible ever present force behind everything that happens and knows everything. He gifted to the human race a gift of free choice. Follow His ways and get rewarded or don't and find death. Eventual eternal peace will arrive to humanity and the era of Moshiach (or Messiah) all Jews will return to the land of Israel to rebuild the Holy Temple in Jerusalem.

Zoroastrianism

(2.6 million) This is the ancient pre-Islamic religion of Iran that survives there in isolated areas and more prosperously in India, where the descendants of Zoroastrian Iranian (Persian) immigrants are known as Parsis or Parsees. Zoroastrianism contains both monotheistic and dualistic features. It likely influenced the other major Western religions. (Retrieved from Britannica.com)

Neo-Paganism

(1 million) Neo-Paganism is any of several spiritual movements that attempt to revive the ancient polytheistic religions of Europe and the Middle East. These movements have a close relationship to ritual magic and modern witchcraft. Neo-Paganism differs from them however in striving to revive authentic pantheons and rituals of ancient cultures, though often in deliberately eclectic and Reconstructionist ways, and by a particularly contemplative and celebrative attitude. Typically people with romantic feelings toward nature and deep ecological concerns, Neo-Pagans center their dramatic and colorful rituals around the changes of the seasons and the personification of nature as full of divine life, as well as the holy days and motifs of the religions by which their own groups are inspired. (Retrieved from Britannica.com)

Unitarian-Universalism

(800,000) Guided by seven principles or otherwise considered strong values or moral guides, these principles are considered "living tradition" of wisdom. The following are the principles outlined in their beliefs: 1) worth and dignity, 2) justice, equity and compassion in human relations, 3) acceptance of one another and encouragement to spiritual growth in our congregations; 4) a free and responsible search for truth and meaning, 5) the right of conscience and the use of the democratic process within our congregations and in society at large, 6) the goal of world community with peace, liberty, and justice for all, 7) respect for the interdependent web of all existence of which we are a part. (Retrieved from UUA.org)

TYPES OF MINISTRY

Hospitality ministries are ministries that take care of the needs of the church itself. Opportunities include organizing and executing potlucks, making bulletins, and working in the church office.

Teaching ministries Those that preach and teach. They include pastors, Sunday school teachers, and religious education directors. Youth groups and Bible studies are teaching ministries, as well.

Outreach ministries Those that minister to a church's community or to the world. Outreach ministers often are missionaries who travel the world to preach. Also include soup kitchens, food pantries, and Habitat for Humanity type environments. Friendly, outgoing people apply within.

Music ministries Those that use music to worship and preach. They include vocal and hand bell choirs, praise bands, and piano or organ playing for weekly services or special events.

Counseling ministries Those that minister to a person's emotional or mental health, in addition to their spirituality. Therapists, counselors, and spiritual directors fall under this category. In the world today this seems to be ever increasing need in our communities for good sound Christian guidance and direction. Within this category we can envision marriage, divorce and even financial counseling being significant.

Thank you Lord
for allowing me to
write this book,
And bless those its
purpose is received upon.
In Jesus name, Amen!